WORLD OF DECEPTION

The Lies, Fraud and Fantasy of Everyday Life

by

Rich Stanit

The Book Tree
San Diego, California

ISBN 978-1-58509-122-5

Cover art: David Dees
Cover layout & design: David Dees
Editor: Kimberly Dillon

Published by
The Book Tree
P O Box 16476
San Diego, CA 92176
www.thebooktree.com

We provide fascinating and educational products to help awaken the public to new ideas and information that would not be available otherwise.
Call 1 (800) 700-8733 for our *FREE BOOK TREE CATALOG*.

Lies are the mortar that bind the savage individual man into the social masonry. —H. G. Wells

All warfare is based on deception. —Sun Tzu

A little inaccuracy sometimes saves tons of explanation. —Saki

A man who uses fraud to overcome his enemy is praised, just as much as he who overcomes his enemy by force.
—Niccolo Machiavelli

We need lies... in order to live. —Friedrich Nietzsche

It is the easiest thing of all to deceive oneself. —Demosthenes

What is a lie? 'Tis but the truth in masquerade. —Lord Byron

The imitator or maker of images knows nothing of true existence, he knows appearances only. —Plato

It is only shallow people who do not judge by appearances.
—Oscar Wilde

The smylere with the knyfe under the cloke. —Geoffrey Chaucer.

O what a tangled web we weave when first we practise to deceive.
—Sir Walter Scott

Force and fraud, are in war the two cardinal virtues.
—Thomas Hobbes

CONTENTS

Chapter One

CAVE ENTRANCE

Plato once suggested that we are all sitting, chained in darkness, at the bottom of a gloomy cave. Our "reality" and only source of education is the dancing shadows on the cave wall in front of us—shadows cast by people just out of sight, who encircle a flickering fire. For us, these lucky elite are the enlightened ones whom we fear, and yet teach us everything we know.

However, if we ever break free of our chains and clamber up through the darkness, past the fire dancers and onto the cave entrance, our perception of reality will begin to change. The brightness will be blinding as we stand out in the real world, but the revelation of what we have been missing will fill our hearts with so much joy that we will desire to return back into the cave to tell others what we have discovered.

Yet this task will be impossible. For as soon as we head back into the cave, the darkness will blind us this time. And if we continue the forbidden descent back down to the place where we were once chained, no amount of persuasion will change the opinions of those who still remain, watching the dancing shadows on the wall.

Moreover, we may well be killed by these troglodytes for speaking of another reality and truer enlightenment. After all, it would not be the first time someone has been killed for trying to tell the truth and educate others. That is the world in which we live, the wide and wonderful word of deception. Whether it is Plato's cave or "The Matrix," there is indeed a reality that is hidden from view. Perhaps it is time we learned to recognise it.

In the 5th century BCE, before being forced to drink a cup of hemlock for corrupting the youth of Athens with his dangerous philosophy, Plato's teacher, Socrates, came to the conclusion that the only thing he knew was that he knew nothing. The paradox of what can be known, what is known, what is not known, and what should not be known, has frustrated mankind ever since.

The logical positivist, A.J. Ayer, tried to solve the problem of knowledge by stating that the only things which should be regarded as being factual and, therefore, worthy of being labelled human knowledge, were those things verifiable by empirical means, or deemed logically true by means of linguistic rules. Unfortunately, none of A.J. Ayer's ideas could be proven empirically and are not tautologically true either and, therefore, not "knowledge" according to his own philosophy.

It therefore seems that if the world's greatest thinkers have difficulty in understanding what is actually known, the rest of us mortals will find it almost impossible.

We have, therefore, become obsessed not by what is, but rather by what is not. Reality for some may be nothing more than illusion to others. Whilst empirical facts often lead to the foundation of knowledge and education, ultimate truth can still be corrupted.

Can things believed by the majority to be the truth actually turn out as lies? Are we all being deceived? The answer is absolutely certain. This is a world of deception where our everyday lives simply could not hope to begin or end without lies and deceit.

So that this book may be understood as I intend it, the terms "deception" and "lies" do not exclusively refer to the misleading actions and words in human interaction. When you are awoken by the sound of a musical alarm clock, the device is not lying to you by mimicking the sound of various instruments. However, your sense of hearing is certainly being deceived.

Every time you eat a bag of roast chicken crisps your sense of taste is being deceived by chemicals and additives designed to mimic cooked poultry. A floral perfume will deceive your sense of smell, whilst make-up will deceive the sense of sight. Moreover, sitting in a dentist's chair, your sense of feeling or touch will thankfully be numbed by local anaesthetic, long before you are deceived into thinking a high revolution drill is not boring through the nerve in your tooth.

Perhaps you are even feeling better after visiting the doctor's office since he has given you a new wonder pill that cures everything. Yet the pill in question could simply be a sugar placebo that the doctor gave you to shut you up. But if you deceive yourself into believing sugar cures all, perhaps it will— especially if you never discover the truth.

People don't really want to know the truth after all. Do we really want to be told about how ugly we are, or that we smell, or that our spouse has been having affairs, or that our friends and family hate us? In such dire circumstances, perhaps the truth would send us to our grave.

On the other hand, you may be a strong enough person to handle the truth and seek to unravel the trail of deception that we have not been allowed to view. If you know what has deceived you and why, it is then up to you regarding what to do with the knowledge.

However, lies and deception can sometimes be very difficult to recognise, as they come in a variety of different shapes and sizes. Some deceit is obvious and some forms of deceit are so well hidden only the sub-conscious mind can detect it, if at all.

This book will, therefore, uncover some everyday deception in its various guises and will also serve to disclose some misinformation disguised as the truth. Some of the blatant falsehood unmasked in the following pages may well be upsetting to those who regarded such as being truthful. However, though my intention is not to insult anyone, be warned that if you are not prepared to consider something which you hold dear as being the product of sheer fabrication, you may well take offense.

Yet truth should not be something to fear, and though its raw state can often bring misery at first, it should also be something to hold close to your heart, for truth is knowledge, and through the proper use of that knowledge there comes wisdom. With wisdom comes spiritual enlightenment and with enlightenment comes peace.

As Aristotle said: "Plato is dear to me, but dearer still is truth."

Chapter Two

DECEPTION IN SOCIETY
AND EVERYDAY LIFE

Although we may not like to admit it, our everyday lives are completely interwoven with deception. Whether this deception is the wearing of make-up or smart clothing to make ourselves look more attractive, or the more drastic action of resorting to plastic surgery and face lifts, it would seem that how things appear is more important to us than how things actually are.

Human Interaction

How we love to deceive others, perhaps even more than ourselves. Each morning we spray on deodorant, splash on after-shave or perfume, thus disguising ourselves in a floral aroma. We mask our bad breath with mint toothpaste and mouthwash, and jump into a suit that makes our shoulders broader than they actually are, or our waist thinner, or our bottom smaller.

If we lose our hair we'll stick on a wig, or dye any remaining hair to make us seem younger. We'll get false or capped teeth, we'll wear a padded bra, we may even have surgery to increase our bust or biceps with saline and silicon implants. But these are examples of physical deception. Greater is our social deception, with a spouse, partners, relations, customers and complete strangers.

When we regularly ask someone how they are, as is the polite custom in society, are we deceiving the subject, the rhetorical question making him believe we actually care what their answer is? And is the person whom we have directed our question at in turn deceiving us by replying that they are fine and have no worries, even if they have had a terrible day? Such little white lies are so common that we may not even regard them as being lies at all, simply a passport to getting through the day without resorting to long and emotional diatribes every time someone says, "Alright mate, how's things?"

However, more often than not, lies are, in fact, rather damaging and make our lives increasingly complicated, especially if we cannot remember what specific lies we have told and to whom. Problems could certainly arise in social circles if we have invented a Walter Mitty background for ourselves, especially if two people to whom we have told a different set of lies suddenly meet up with each other.

These people could be friends from separate social classes or life philosophies, or perhaps partners whom we are married to or courting simultaneously, yet also two people whom we had never imagined would meet, who have the chance to put all the pieces of our identity puzzle together. Furthermore, this situation could even result in a criminal prosecution if we have invented a false education or employment background to get a well paid job or a position of responsibility.

There was a case where a local government councillor was imprisoned when an office worker noted the details of the councillor's framed degrees, placed proudly on the wall behind her desk. Her degrees were in medicine and law, which would be impossible to gain within the time period which the councillor claimed they had been completed. Apparently one of her degrees had been purchased from a bogus internet university, selling instant degrees in any subject or field of research.

Recognising conflicting dates or information on official documents is perhaps a more empirically, easier way of detecting deception, but recognising someone lying is a far more difficult task when it comes to analysing a person's words or behaviour.

Although lie-detector machines have been used for decades to help police interrogate suspected criminals, the polygraph has been fooled on several occasions, and cannot, therefore, be fully trusted. The problem with the lie-detector is that it relies on changes to a person's breathing patterns, blood pressure, heart rate and sweat production, the theory being that such changes in these variables arise from an emotional reaction to questions concerning guilt or honesty.

However, the data that such devices gather can be voided if questions which a subject gives answers to are known to be truthful, yet provoke the same changes to his heart rate and blood pressure as a lie. In such cases where there is no difference in a subject's reaction to questions, be he telling the truth or lying, the polygraph data cannot be trusted.

Moreover, a trick that is sometimes used to assure the failure of the lie-detector is for a subject to bite his tongue or push down on a drawing pin in his shoe when giving an honest response. The pain of such an action will imitate the same physiological response as when he is deliberately lying.

With recent research on polygraph tests showing that they have a 30% chance of being erroneous, the American Psychological Association made a statement admitting that the lie detector is ineffective.

New technology for detecting when an individual is lying is currently being developed. Among these technologies are devices that track small changes to the brain's electrical patterns when we lie or think of deceptive "event-related potentials." The development of heat sensing cameras that allow us to see a temperature change around the eyes of someone who is lying is also in progress.

Until a reliable lie detector is developed, human "gut reaction" may still be the best way to recognise a liar. However, criminal psychologists are investigating the phenomenon of micro-expressions, or those brief subconscious facial movements that we cannot control. The quick raising of eyebrows in a look of fear, or a down-turned frown of the mouth in sadness being only two micro-expressions that may indicate that lies are being told.

Behavioural psychologists and body language experts alike have investigated the science of recognising lies, yet a foolproof deception formula has yet to be discovered. Although nothing more than educated conjecture, there are certain observations about deceivers that give us general guidelines. For example we have all heard that liars have a nasty habit of scratching their noses when they spin a yarn, but there are many other clues to deceit that are not commonly recognised.

A person who is being questioned about a lie they have told will turn away from their inquisitor and do anything to avoid eye contact. Yet, conversely, they will look you straight in the eye when pretending to recall a memory of a past event. If they are lying about such a memory their eyes will not flicker. However, if they are truthfully recollecting a past event their eyes should quickly flicker upwards.

A liar will also place symbolic barriers in front of them, like a cushion, a bag or a cup of coffee, etc. They might anchor their hands deeply in their pockets to disguise nervous shaking, and they will often repeat the question they have just been asked, stalling for time as they try to think up a believable answer. The answer that they eventually offer may well be welded to an unnecessary and extremely emotional reaction, such as becoming very angry or quiet and withdrawn. Bizarrely, a further indication of potential deceit could be the overuse of the expressions: "to be honest" or "in truth."

Deceit in relationships is perhaps the biggest emotional minefield in human interaction, yet here, too, there are some general rules for detecting infidelity or lies. If a partner rushes into the shower as soon as they return home there is a good chance that they are washing away the scent of another person, and symbolically baptising themselves clean of guilt.

Moreover, if a partner makes light of an unusual circumstance, they may be up to no good. A boyfriend who says he has to spend a weekend away with his company, whilst in the middle of discussing the week's shopping list, is probably hiding the fact he intends to organise a little fling. If a partner is questioned about suspicious activities, any gross exaggeration or overt sarcasm in their answer usually heralds a lie.

A wife could be asked where she was all night and why she was late arriving home. If she replies that she was having sex with an entire football team before being abducted by aliens, chances are there may be some truth in her statement. Forget the aliens and remember that even if she only had sex with one football player, it would still mean infidelity. A partner who is lying may also be unable to provide many facts about their statement, or show evidence to back up what they say, or produce notes or minutes of the meeting they said they attended, etc.

Aside from passively trying to detect when someone is lying, a person can also cajole and tease the truth from a deceiver by feeding them leading questions. Similar to Machiavelli's observation about archers aiming at targets high above enemy soldiers in order that their arrows should rain down on those soldiers within a certain range, such is the ploy to calmly accept a lie far greater than the one suspected.

If a policeman seems to excuse a criminal's suspected act of murder, perhaps saying that these sorts of things happen all the time, perhaps the criminal would seem happier to confess his real crime. After all, if the policeman didn't seem too bothered about the murder, he's hardly likely to be more concerned with a mugging or a robbery.

"So you killed someone in cold blood, well nobody's perfect, maybe they deserved to die, don't worry, ...oh just before I forget, how many wallets did you steal last week?"

When confronting a partner who is suspected of having an affair, the inquisitor should begin the conversation by saying that they understand why their partner would want to have several affairs. Moreover, that they have proof of such infidelities. A guilty partner may then confess to only one fling, thinking that their partner already knows of the adultery and does not particularly care.

"How many men have you slept with honey? I've been a bad husband. I'm sorry. Don't worry, I won't shoot you if you tell me all their names."

"It was just one man. His name is ...."

BANG!!!

The deception that the guilty will not be punished if they confess their crimes, but are punished when they do, is a popular tactic of religious and civil prosecutors world-wide. It is an effective ploy but will not generally work on the same person more than once. Never punish your own children, for example, if you have promised them immunity from such if they tell the truth. You will only classically condition them to lie as a matter of routine.

No matter what their crime, if they have told the truth about it, they should be shown at least some mercy or a degree of patience. Deceitful children, on the other hand, should be dealt with severely and discouraged from lying at all costs. The only caveat to the latter recommendation is that if you, the reader, beat or abuse your children regardless of what they say, you can't blame them for lying. Moreover, if you regularly hit your children then you are lying to yourself about being a good parent.

Politics

How do you know when a politician is lying? ...His lips are moving.

Politicians delight in evading the truth and fear giving an honest answer. Aside from authoring party manifestos, politicians can often be at their most deceitful during a televised debate with other professional liars. The rhetoric and verbal bovine faeces that such sessions produce are not only annoying to viewers, but generally spew forth such cascades of sham and fabrication as to rival the worst utterances of Satan himself (if Satan existed, that is).

Politicians trapped in such publicly broadcast positions often begin their reply to unwelcome questions by saying how great the question was, before answering the question they *wanted* to be asked. Moreover, if their curious reply is in turn questioned as to its relevance, the politician will begin his or her long, defensive and well rehearsed speech, usually about how they should be allowed to finish what they were saying, and how they were silent when it was previously the turn of someone else to lie to the public.

Aside from religious institutions and texts, most of the world's lies are found crouching under the cloaks of devious politicians. From the days of early sophistry in the classical world, politicians and lawyers have continued to make an art form of lying, and have amassed rather large sums of money in the process. Politics has, therefore, nothing to do with helping the people who vote for politicians, but is entirely about politicians helping themselves.

Those politicians who enter the filthy profession under the banner of "conviction" and "strong belief" often find themselves without even the slightest hint of support from the masses. Furthermore, politics is a game where the players try to solve nagging problems, without worrying about the long term effects of their solutions. Politicians make deals with sinners, and they make deals with saints. Politicians make deals with anyone who can give them what they need.

Although Aristotle and Herodotus detailed many dirty political tricks used by the tyrants of ancient Greece, it is Niccolo Machiavelli who is remembered for being one of the fathers of political science and "spin." In his two polemical observations of Roman and European politics, *The Prince* and *The Discourses*, Machiavelli gave the world a formula for gaining and keeping power, even if it was preserved at all costs, regardless of who was hurt, overthrown or killed.

Although both of the Florentine statesman's books were written circa 1513, they were successfully banned by the pope for several years after. Apparently the pontiff did not want the dreadful information in these books circulating in the public domain. No wonder, seeing as one of Machiavelli's archetypal bastards, which he regarded as the ultimate prince, was the son of Pope Alexander VI. This man was Cesare Borgia, a cruel and ruthless

Cardinal of the church who murdered most of his political enemies, his brother included, whilst having an incestuous affair with his own sister.

Whilst I would love to detail all of Machiavelli's ideas with regard to deception in politics, I think they are best presented in his own works. However, I will give a brief description of just some of his theories, especially in connection with modern spin-doctoring, or the practise of making politicians look good and enabling them to escape criticism by blaming their wrongful actions on someone else.

In the United Kingdom, late 20th Century politics saw the metamorphosis and rise of the all-improved, new-recipe, best-ever New Labour party—a party that found success when it gave up its commitment to socialism, ditching its nationalised industry and services anchor known as Clause 4.

This despite the fact that such nationalised industry and services guarantees high standards, correct safety procedures in the workplace (proper equipment used in factories, etc.). And most of all, that people come before profit. Moreover, nationalised industry ensures that jobs cannot be sacrificed on a whim, that a worker's wage increases according to inflation, and that goods and services will not be charged at a level beyond what most people are willing to pay, unlike the private sector. The deception here being that the government cares about industry, services and jobs more than their own, of course.

Sadly the UK has followed the American model of profits before people and, as such, has created an environment where commuters pay through the nose to take a train to work each morning, a train that will be late, filthy and poorly maintained. The same commuters may return home at night to find their water supply has been cut off, a result of the exceptionally ill managed and criminal exploits of water suppliers who live in a country known the world over for its rain!

New Labour has subsequently become associated with the parasitic bloodsucking values of old Conservatism, but with the added stigma of being routinely dishonest as a party policy. For example, the first emperor of New Labour being Tony Blair, a once articulate and intelligent Prime Minster with a grin as wide as the English Channel. Now Blair has been shown to be a devious and calculating politician who will be remembered for his mistake of supporting U.S. President George W. Bush in his attempts to invade and destroy several countries in the Middle East.

Unfortunately for New Labour, all of its minions are not quite so adept at lying as its top prime ministerial advisors. The department of public transport once had a spin doctor who claimed that September the 11th was "a good day," as the news from New York would camouflage governmental blunders in the UK. The spin doctor was, of course, criticised in Parliament and the media alike, but what she had to say was essentially correct, at least by Machiavellian standards. In *The Prince*, Machiavelli recommended that bad news or unwelcome policies be delivered into the public forum all at once:

"Injuries should be inflicted all at the same time, for the less they are tasted, the less they offend; and benefits should be distributed a bit at a time in order that they may be savoured fully."

This recommendation sprang from his belief that the public have short memories, in all matters other than the loss of their money, and possess little understanding of politics. To bombard the masses with complicated issues of government, and expect them to understand what they meant, would prove to be too great a task.

This example can be demonstrated in the case of the management of big businesses, where a new appointee to the role will often cut 50% of a company's spending within the first 100 days, and initiate all major changes within this time. This, of course, may result in redundancies being created. But if the drastic measure works, and the company's profits increase, those remaining in the company's employ will soon forget the absence of their former colleagues, especially if the loss of such work-mates in fact results in moderate wage rises for those who we not condemned to the dole queue.

In his advice on how to be a good politician, or prince, Machiavelli suggests that the candidate in question must learn how to be bad. Moreover, as men are fooled by appearances, he should look the part he wants to play. This could mean looking handsome, calm and intelligent, in control of a given situation, as John F. Kennedy looked on his famous television debate with the rival presidential candidate of the day, Richard Nixon. He could also give the appearance of being a god fearing, merciful or religious man, who seemingly has high moral values. Whether or not a politician actually possesses these values is beside the point, that he appears as if he does is all that is required.

Amusingly, Machiavelli was, himself, Machiavellian and played to both sides, by giving support to principalities in one book and to republics in another. He thus deceives us with unashamed ambivalence, by holding two conflicting opinions at the same time. His paradoxical dialectic, therefore, allows him to escape too much criticism, by wriggling out of having a concrete opinion on anything.

On one hand he tells the prince that he should try not to be hated by the masses, not to be effeminate or irresolute, to practise the art of war and to avoid flatters. Meanwhile, on the other hand, he tells those around the prince to offer him gifts, which will please him, and to laugh at all his jokes, and therefore to be the very flatterers whom he has informed the prince to be rid of. Thus, there is no single set of rules or guidelines that will suit all situations in politics or business. When it comes to the art of deceit, if Machiavelli could not come up with all of the answers, no one can.

Although some commentators would have us believe that Niccolo Machiavelli was an immoral man who wrote wicked guidebooks for dictators such as Hitler and Mussolini, it could be argued that he was simply a keen observer of the dreadful behaviour found in political fields. Moreover, the English language itself continues to deceive us by claiming that a Machiavellian politician is "destitute of political morality"(Chambers), rather than one who gives a good example to the masses by performing merciful deeds or initiating brave, intelligent, decisive actions, all of which Machiavelli recommended.

Moving on to a discussion of world politics, we tend to encounter much conflict and deception, especially concerning the polarity between ideology, culture, sovereignty and national security. A variety of countries throughout the world have appalling histories of human rights abuses, usually derived from suppression of information and freedom of speech.

The USA, the apparent land of the free, has been just as guilty as anywhere else in silencing the truth and successfully deceiving both Americans and the rest of the world on many occasions. For example, border patrols in California will tell you that something must be done to keep the high number of illegal immigrants out of their state and country. However, in actuality, nearly half of all farm workers in America are illegally employed Mexicans, and as such they help to boost the American economy by working for a pittance in their almost slave-like existence.

Deception in the US is common even from the early days of elementary school, where children are taught that Christopher Columbus discovered America in 1492. This is of course nonsense! There were already people living in the Americas who had truly discovered the continents after crossing the Bering Strait from Asia, thousands of years before Christ's birth. Moreover, the Viking Leif Eriksson is thought to have also sailed to America circa 1000 AD, nearly 500 years before any other Europeans.

The deception surrounding the so-called discovery of the New World is further complicated by the unusual move of naming it after Florentine navigator Amerigo Vespucci, despite the fact that he never set foot on the North American mainland (neither did Columbus).

The name America is actually derived from the surname of the financial sponsor and patron of John Cabot, a Bristol customs official called Richard Amerik. John Cabot (real name; Giovanni Caboto), was the Italian explorer who sailed to North America in 1497, under the commission of King Henry VII.

As is the tradition, surnames usually inspire the name of a country, state or city, not Christian or first names. Therefore, if America was really named after Amerigo Vespucci the county would be called "Vespuccia."

Aside from the muddled history of America's name, the next deception that U.S. schoolchildren encounter is that their country is the best in the world, and that communists are their arch enemy. Whilst there's nothing essentially wrong with being patriotic, if obsessive jingoism replaces political and cultural fact, such a practise can only result in the creation of a rather insular nation. This situation is clarified by the fact that less than 21% of Americans own passports to travel overseas.

Americans may like to call their home "the land of the free" and "the home of the brave," but God's country is not without fault. America is the world's greatest polluter of the atmosphere, partly as a result of failing to reduce carbon dioxide and "greenhouse gas" emissions, which are the main cause of global warming. America also wastes more resources than any other country.

Plagued with drugs, gangs and guns, America has the highest crime rates of any developed country. Not including unintentional homicide in street fights or barroom brawls, or accidental homicide deriving from careless gun discharges and shooting incidents, around 9 people in 100,000 are brutally murdered every year, whilst 35 women in 100,000 are raped.

The social divisions between the rich and the poor is widening in the USA. The rich are getting richer; the poor are getting poorer. Around seven and a half million people are unemployed, whilst nearly 40 million people do not have any health insurance. It is estimated that around 30 million people live in dire poverty, whilst the U.S. has an increasing prison population of over two million inmates. So around 1 out of every 142 Americans is incarcerated.

However, perhaps the biggest deception that America has pulled off is that the rest of the world is in its debt, whilst quite the opposite is true. America owes the World Bank and other countries more than any other country, nearly ten trillion dollars. Speaking of debt, the choices that capitalism in the land of the free provides seems to have given Americans too many temptations to resist. As such, credit card and national consumer debt lies at nearly $1.7 trillion dollars.

To paraphrase the late comedian Bill Hicks, Americans are free to buy what they are told to buy and free to believe what they are told to believe.

As far as hating communists, or perhaps fearing them, this is a very unfair discrimination. Despite the success of the Red Army in capturing Berlin and proving to be the most feared of Germany's enemies, 27 million Soviets died as a result of WWII. Russia, therefore, was the most important ally of the free world, helping civilised nations win the war against fascism.

Despite helping to defeat Hitler, after WWII America wanted the world to think of the Russians as being the big bad enemy. But the fear created by the "Cold War" and the nuclear weapons once present in Cuba was entirely of America's making. Prior to 1958, Batista's Cuba was one of extreme divisions between the rich and poor, where most islanders were near to starving, uneducated and illiterate. Fidel Castro's revolution not only changed the foundation of Cuba's executive body, it also changed the fortunes of its people. Thus, Cuba became the cornucopia of highly educated doctors and radiation scientists it is today.

However, the fact that Cuba is a communist country is also its greatest hindrance to success—not because of communism itself, but because

American trade embargoes have crippled Cuba to the point of architectural decay and massive shortages of resources. It seems the great capitalist nation could not bear to see a small communist island be prosperous and happy so near to its shores.

I wonder whether the United States will ease into a friendlier relationship with Cuba, now that the Caribbean island has discovered a huge supply of oil, just waiting to be drilled, pumped and sold.

Another good chance for renewed diplomatic and economic relations with Cuba could be the influence and policies of Barack Obama, the 44th President of the United States.

Many countries around the world are praying that President Obama will be the incarnation of Dr. Martin Luther King, and a man of peace and rational thought. African countries hope Obama will give them greater financial assistance as he is a black man. Asian countries hope he will be their friend, as he once attended school in Indonesia. Whilst European countries see Obama as an intelligent politician with new ideas, who could bring stability and peace to the world.

The election of Barack Obama as America's first black President is like a breath of fresh air and a truly wonderful moment in history. But we should all be cautious about celebrating too quickly. Mr Obama is, after all, a politician and a lawyer—two professions not known for their wealth of honesty.

President Obama was elected for many reasons, not least of which was the overwhelming desire to change the direction in which George W. Bush and the Republican Party were steering America. It could be argued that black people and ethnic minorities voted for the black man. Young people voted for the young man. Women voted for the handsome man, and men voted for an inspirational male role model.

But remember that all that glisters is not gold. I, too, like Obama and hope he proves all his critics and detractors wrong by solving the global economic crisis and ending the conflicts in Iraq and Afghanistan. But I can't ignore the saying, "If it's too good to be true, it probably is." Just because Obama is black, it is no guarantee that he will be a black-friendly President. Indeed, it could be argued that as the leader of the free world he should treat everyone equally, regardless of colour or ethnicity. Furthermore, is it perhaps rather insulting to suggest that black people only voted for him because he is black, and he should not feel obligated to cut the African American community a bigger slice of the pie than anyone else. He should indeed give some pie to those who are currently starving.

In Kenya there were great celebrations to mark Obama's election success, as the people there imagined that, as Obama's father was born in Kenya, they would soon reap the benefit of a family connection. But Kenyans are forgetting that President Obama is American and must put the interests of the United States before all other nations, family connection or not.

Indeed, the Kenyan link may prove to be a thorn in Obama's side. If fundamentalist Muslims agree that the President is now a Christian, then in fact he is an apostate and must be killed. Technically, Obama was born a Muslim, as his father was a Muslim. Islamic fundamentalists would therefore say that he has turned his back on Mohammad. Of course, the same religious maniacs may also want him dead as he is simply the U.S. President, giving no other reason for their unsavoury wish to be granted.

Aside from the similarities between President Obama and Dr. Martin Luther King, there are also similarities between Obama and JFK—both popular and attractive young men. Both with ambition and both seeming to represent a force for good. But let us hope that Obama is not the incarnation of JFK, as the assassinated playboy President was actually quite inexperienced and ineffectual. JFK also made some dreadful mistakes—the disastrous "Bay of Pigs" being just one of note.

The deception of Barack Obama is therefore that we are all projecting noble characteristics onto him, as an idol and messianic figure who will bring us salvation. But we are also ignoring the fact that Obama says he is religious, a supporter of Israel, and that he is unafraid to go to war with Iran and even Pakistan if he has to. We don't need yet another religious Zionist with a war fetish!

As U.S. President, Barack Obama has both inherited the problems left by his predecessors and the title of Commander in Chief of the U.S. Armed Forces. Obama's story begins with a brilliant opening chapter, but in the political pressure cooker of the White House, absolute power may quickly corrupt and distort his benevolent ideals, and there may not be the happy ending which we all desire. So let's just wait and see what happens before we make Obama a saint.

Conspiracy Theories

Although Machiavelli pointed out that there have been few grand conspiracies ever to be successful, his conclusion was made after he had been tortured on the rack, accused of being part of a conspiracy himself.

However, modern technology and communications networks now make cover-ups far easier than in Machiavelli's day. And though "Occam's Razor" may point out that the truth is usually more simplistic than complicated conspiracies existing, we should not believe that conspiracies do not exist. Take note of Hitler's chilling maxim expressed in *Mein Kampf*:

"The broad mass of a nation... will more easily fall victim to a big lie than to a small one."

Therefore, conspiracies absolutely depend on the public's belief in simple truth being more probable than cover-ups, or, in fact, public apathy regarding the matter.

Conspiracy theories, of which there are plenty, never fail to fascinate us, whether they are believable or not. Everything from a Masonic New World Order of shape-shifting reptilian vampires ruling our planet, to Elvis being alive and well have been suggested.

It is one thing to be fascinated by an idea of a cover-up or conspiracy, and quite another to take the leap of faith towards complete belief in such. After all, even though we may suspect a conspiracy theory is actually the truth, we do not want to confirm that the powers that run the planet are capable of such uncivilized acts of assassination and corruption.

Yet even though we may not wish to believe we are being lied to by governments, police and other trusted agencies in society, it is time we woke up and faced reality. There is deception everywhere, especially in the world's governments and law enforcement institutions. However, the belief in shape-shifting reptiles being elected to government is not so much a leap of faith, but rather more a sign of one's mental instability.

Over recent years the main supporter of the idea that reptilian "Illuminati" ("enlightened ones") are in control of the planet is Englishman David Icke. An ex-football player (European term, meaning soccer) and TV sports commentator, Icke has become one of the leading figures on the conspiracy theory public speaking circuit. His arguments and observations about symbols of 'The New World Order" are plentiful and often eye opening.

However, despite all the great observations he has made, he has also stated that he is the son of God and that the end of the world is nigh, almost as often as Jehovah's Witnesses. So unless Mr. Icke can provide some empirical evidence for his reptile royalty theory, I suggest we all place it on the shelf, next to our DVD collection of "V" the TV mini-series of the 1980s, which first articulated the fascist reptilian overlord idea.

One of the most notorious conspiracy theories of the modern era is the 1963 assassination of PresidentJohn F. Kennedy in Dallas, which has become more of a mainstream belief than a conspiracy theory. It is fair to say that most of us believe that J.F.K. was not killed by Lee Harvey Oswald, and was instead assassinated by a U.S. state security bureau or the Mafia, the reason for his assassination being that he wanted to withdraw troops from Vietnam before the war escalated. Or that he crossed powerful gangsters who had helped both President Kennedy and his brother, Robert, rise to power. Or that he was about to change the entire monetary system and get rid of the Federal Reserve.

He may also have been killed because his easy going playboy image was mocking the serious politics of the Congressional stuffed shirts. His lover, Marilyn Monroe, who it is thought was assassinated with a rectal insertion of poison, may also have been killed to protect the image of the presidency. Of course, this is all assuming that she was pregnant with the child of one of the Kennedy brothers, both of whom she was sleeping with.

The death of Diana, Princess of Wales, was possibly the result of a planned car crash in Paris, August 1997, for the same reasons as Monroe's death—to protect an institution more important than the life of any one individual. In this case, that institution was the British Royal Family. Therefore, Diana may have been assassinated because of her plans to marry Dodi Al Fayed, the rich Muslim son of Mohammad Al Fayed. Such a marriage could have provided Muslim step-brothers for the future King.

In this age of multi-culture, it may be imagined that a marriage of mixed faiths may not be damaging in the slightest to the British monarchy, and in the most part this would be true. Indeed, such a marriage may have helped to bring Western and Middle-Eastern cultures together in some way. However, this is assuming that both cultures want to be brought together.

Whilst the official conclusion remains that the crash was the result of bad driving by an incompetent alcoholic, there is mounting evidence to suggest foul play. In October 2003, the British press again ignited the flame of conspiracy by reporting that Paul Burrell, Diana's former butler, had a letter handwritten by the Princess of Wales, detailing her own suspicions that the brakes on her car had been tampered with to deliberately cause her death in a road traffic accident. Whether this was paranoia on Diana's part or a morbid premonition of her fate, we will never know.

What raises further suspicion about a conspiracy are the facts surrounding her mysterious death. Prior to taking what was to be a short vacation in Paris, Diana had promised the media a revelation that would shock the world. Could this revelation have been that Prince Charles had been witnessed engaging in a homosexual act? This revelation, if true, would have had dire consequences for the future of the monarchy. Some claim she was pregnant with Dodi's child. However, the revelation, whatever it may have been, has yet to be fully uncovered.

The first reports of the crash in a Paris underpass were from eyewitnesses who saw motorbikes and a white Fiat Uno chasing Diana's car. They also saw the princess alive and walking to an ambulance with some help. Some witnesses even reported hearing a loud explosion, possibly from a small explosive device in Diana's Mercedes.

However, despite these reports, the official understanding of her death is that she was fatally injured by a high-speed crash into the thirtieth pillar of the underpass, and that she died along with her lover Dodi and driver, Henri Paul. All deaths were a result of not wearing seat belts.

There was another passenger in the car, however—Diana's bodyguard, Trevor Rees-Jones, a man who has suffered amnesia ever since, and apparently cannot remember any details concerning the accident.

Conspiracy theorists, however, refuse to believe the hazy conclusions of the French police, and feel unsatisfied by the results of the 2007 British-led inquest to establish the truth of Diana's death.

The inquest, which was held in both England and France, retraced Diana's last movements in Paris and assembled experts and witnesses alike to once again explain what happened on the night of August 31, 1997.

Whatever the truth of the tragic event, there is a certain stink regarding some of the "facts" surrounding the matter. For example, initial photographs of the crash site were taken by a French journalist, who apparently committed suicide after he discovered that the negatives and copies of such had been stolen from his flat. The British press said they did not buy the photographs out of respect for Diana, an obvious lie, as the British press are renowned for their total lack of morality.

The driver of the white Fiat seen chasing Diana's Mercedes was thought to have been tracked down by private detectives hired my Mohammed Al-Fayed, but the man in question committed suicide by setting fire to himself before he could be properly questioned about his part in the accident. His name was James Andason, and aside from his freelance work as a photographer, he also worked for MI6 (British Intelligence).

An examination of Henry Paul's blood sample showed that Diana's driver was three times over the legal limit for drunk driving, and he also had an unusually high level of carbon monoxide in his system. It is said that Henry Paul, when not driving for a living, also worked for MI6.

Could their employers in British intelligence have silenced both Andason and Paul?

Other facts that are the author of much debate about Diana's "accident" are that paparazzi motorbike and moped riders are blamed for forcing the princess's driver to accelerate in an attempt to outrun them. Yet this should have been easy to achieve in such a high performance car as a Mercedes. Could the car have been tampered with as Diana suggested? After all, there was indeed an opportunity for this as the car had been stolen only three months previously, and had its onboard computer removed.

After the accident, in an attempt to shift the blame from any fault that the car may have had, Mercedes sent a team of experts to examine the wreckage. However, they were denied access to the mangled vehicle by French authorities.

As for the reports of an explosion, French authorities removed any evidence of this when they ordered that the underpass be sprayed with detergent only hours after the crash, making a concise forensic examination of the crash site impossible. It has also been reported that video cameras that normally record this portion of the highway were suddenly not working during the accident, so that no video footage of the accident exists.

The final piece of information that may arouse a great deal of suspicion is that it took Diana's ambulance 1 hour 10 minutes to travel a distance of three miles to the nearest hospital. Why? After all, she was still alive when she was pulled from the wreckage of her car, and may have stood some possibility of survival if she had been rushed to a hospital's operating theatre.

When she was sadly pronounced dead, a decision was made to embalm her body almost immediately. The embalming was said to have been carried out as a way of ensuring that her beauty was not lost in decomposition. After all, even as a corpse Princess Diana would still be in the public eye. However, it could be argued that embalming Diana would also make it impossible to prove she was pregnant or the victim of poisoning, poison perhaps being administered in the back of the slow ambulance, as a backup plan to her failing to die in the car crash.

Like all good conspiracy theories, the details of Diana's death are further complicated by the attempts to explain why she may have been killed. Two rather ambitious suggestions are that her death was an occult sacrifice to the pagan goddess Diana the Huntress, or that she was assassinated by arms dealers who were bitter about her anti-landmine campaign.

However, for Christians, a more compelling motive for Diana's possible murder can also be found. The Princess of Wales came from a bloodline of aristocrats from the Royal house of Stuart. The Stuarts were, in turn, related to the French Merovingian Royal Family. Although the Merovingian rule ended before the first millennium, their own bloodline is itself the subject of much controversy and debate.

The Knights Templar, who led crusades against the Muslim world for over two hundred years, also protected a secret that was eventually enough to spell their destruction by Pope Clement V. The Templar treasure, written of in medieval texts, was not the Holy Grail as it was supposed, but something far more threatening to the Church of Rome. This was "Sangraal," which apparently referred to the cup that Jesus sipped from at the Last Supper, thus producing a grail that would have magical or healing qualities.

However, it was not a Holy Grail that the Knights protected, but the holy blood, or "Sang Real," which was either contained in the Grail itself, the "blood of Christ," similar to communion wine, or a bloodline of Christ. In other words, the Merovingian were possibly descendants of Christ's siblings or even his children, offspring who were a result of Christ actually having been rescued from the Cross and perhaps taken to France, where he lived out his days in Rennes-Le-Chateau.

The holy bloodline may also have arisen from Christ's marriage to Mary Magdalene, an idea expressed in Dan Brown's novel, *The Da Vinci Code*.

If a Merovingian church were to be founded that would rival the Church of Rome, it would be essential for the pope to wipe out all traces of such an institution. After all, religious consumers would certainly choose to join a church whose patrons were actually of Christ's bloodline, rather than that of his followers.

And so, the Roman Catholic Church destroyed the mighty, accusing them of worshipping Baphomet, the goat of Mendes, and performing Satanic and homosexual rituals. Whilst it is nonsense to accuse the Crusader Knights of worshipping a goat-headed incarnation of the Devil, there is, however, some truth in the statement that "they worshipped Baphomet."

The Crusades (wars of the cross) were fought in Middle Eastern locations, such as Jerusalem, deemed essential properties of the Christian world. These bloody wars spanned a period of nearly two-hundred years. Over this time, Christian Knights walked the same ground and drank the same water as their Muslim Saracen foes. Therefore, it is probable that captors, prisoners, negotiators, diplomats, holy men and warriors shared the philosophy of their different religions with each other, as each side asked themselves, "Why are we fighting?"—a question every soldier asks after battle.

As the philosophy of Islam became known by the Crusaders, it is possible that there were Christians who were attracted to the Muslim way of thinking as a more disciplined and rigid system of worship, suited to the life of a soldier.

Therefore, the Knights who worshipped Baphomet were actually Muslim converts or Christians who had sympathy for the philosophy expressed in the Qur'an. Indeed, "Baphomet" may be a French/English bastardised translation or mispronunciation of "Mohammad" (Mahommet).

If the greatest of the crusaders could be brutally dispatched by the pope's decree, then Diana, Princess of Wales could easily have fallen victim to the same plot. Not because she was a threat to the Catholic Church, but because Christ's bloodline would have been mixed with that of a Saracen. As the monarch of Britain is traditionally known as the "defender of the faith" (Christian), it seems likely that Diana's attempts to marry into an Islamic household would have aroused the anger of those who were anti-Islamic and powerful enough to have her killed.

Perhaps these are the same people who support the idea of white supremacy, based of the concept of Aryans being the evolutionary "over-men" predicted by Nietzsche, and thus the German master race. If this is true it is unfortunate for those who have lived, died and killed for the belief. The truth is that the Aryans are not, in fact, the direct ancestors of Nordic, Germanic or Saxon races. How embarrassing for the Nazis.

Even more embarrassing for modern-day white supremacists is the fact that if Hitler had won the Second World War, they would not be welcomed into the ranks of the Nazi party. Fat, bald, tattooed, uneducated, working class "white trash" are kidding themselves if they think they resemble Nietzsche's "supermen," and satisfy the aim of Hitler's policy on eugenics. Such thuggish morons would, I'm sure, have shared floor space in the showers alongside Jews, gypsies, black and gay people.

The Nazis tried to breed a new generation of Nordic/Germanic heroes for the rest of the planet to serve and worship as gods. They were ideally blonde, blue-eyed, physically fit and beautiful Germans who were cultured, educated, and who followed the noble warrior values of the Teutonic Knights. The iconography of this German "master race" would resemble the operas of Wagner, based on the tales of Arthurian legend, and their uniformity and discipline would bring order to the world, creating a new civilisation—powerful, strong and, sadly, also perverted, corrupt and entirely evil!

I'd like to ask white supremacists such as the Ku Klux Klan and other Christian "white power" groups throughout America, Britain and Europe, just what connection they think they have with the image of the German "master race," or indeed with Christianity. Overweight, uneducated, tattooed, ape-like, beer swilling hooligans wouldn't satisfy the membership criteria to be a vomit rag on the floor of a Munich beer-hall in Nazi Germany, never mind entering the ranks of the Vermacht.

Despite Hitler being a Catholic, the Nazis were not a Christian organisation. They practised occult ceremonies that related more to the pagan gods of Scandinavia and ancient Rome, and worshipped Hitler as the new Christ. Remember a Nazi would have found the idea of Jesus being the son of God as distasteful, as Christ was Jewish and would have had dark skin and Arabic features—an image far removed from Medieval Christian portraits. Moreover, the Nazis also held the belief that their ancestors came from the highly advanced civilisation of Atlantis, not the redneck bars of Atlanta, Georgia.

Thus "white power" is a slogan chanted by people that true Nazis would disown, whilst "Heil Hitler" is a slogan chanted by those whom everyone else should disown.

If Princess Diana had knowledge of something that the Royal Family wished she had not, they may have wanted to ensure Diana's silence by killing her, a warning to the current monarchy. If their vile deed is ever proven, the British people could quickly replace them with members of the House of Hanover, who have just as much claim to the throne as the "Windsors" (aka Saxe-Coburg-Gotha). Indeed the 21st Century may even welcome the dawn of a new British republic, with a president to replace the king or queen.

Returning from British conspiracy theories to American, it is interesting that most Americans and some from other countries regard the U.S. military as being the best in the world. In reality, however, the U.S. armed forces are not nearly as competent as they are portrayed in Hollywood films, or by the horribly subjective American media.

Members of the National Guard, who were deployed across America following the attacks of September 11th, were trusted to patrol streets and airports with semi-automatic assault weapons. Yet these are the same part-time troops that train, on average, one or two days a month, and find great difficulty in marching in unison, never mind the mastery of combat skills and the safe handling of weapons.

So why is it that the American public trusts the National Guard to save their lives when it can't even march properly? The reason is that the American public is deceiving itself into believing its armed forces, police and intelligence services are on the ball, highly trained, highly motivated and highly informed. However, the truth is quite the reverse.

The Vietnam War was lost despite the mighty U.S. Air Force dumping thousands of tons of napalm and explosives on the small Asian county. On the ground, the U.S. Army has a terrible record for being under trained and overly keen to fire their vast arsenal of weapons. Unfortunately, their trigger-happy barrage has often been aimed at American allies, such as the British, who suffered many casualties of "friendly fire" in the Gulf and Iraq wars.

The U.S. Navy does not escape ridicule either, apparently having blown up a passenger aircraft en route to Paris from New York, killing 230 people. The TWA 800 conspiracy theory flies in the face of the FBI's official conclusion to the accident investigation. The FBI reported the accident a result of engine failure, despite 183 witnesses swearing that they saw a missile hit the plane, missile fragments being found amongst the plane's wreckage and a photo of a missile heading towards the plane being published in a French magazine. The truth may be that a drone target missile strayed beyond the range of a Navy training vessel, which was meant to shoot it down during routine target practice.

It is not only the U.S. military that has inspired many conspiracy theories over the years. There has also been rumour about cover-ups of UFO landings and arms deals with terrorists, etc. NASA, too, has been the subject of perhaps one of the most important conspiracies in history. I refer, of course, to the moon landings, a conspiracy that, if found to be true, will be a rather depressing revelation for the world's scientific community to accept.

America of the 1960's saw many cultural changes, but the one thing that remained constant throughout the decade was the desire to overtake Russian invention and scientific advances, lest the Communists enjoy technical dominance of the entire planet. The desire to get one up on the "Commies" was such that the United States may have pulled off the biggest fraud of all time, other than religious leaders making people believe that we are in communion with God.

Despite the fact that a journey to the moon would require astronauts to protect themselves with six feet of lead to safely pass through the Van Allen belts of Earth's upper atmosphere, it is also hard to believe that no astronaut has died of radiation sickness. Presumably NASA expects us to believe that their "special" space suits and flimsy tinfoil-clad lunar modules protected them. But this aside, it is obvious from NASA's own movies and pictures of the moon landings (most now officially misplaced) that there is something fishy going on.

In NASA's films and photographs, shadows are observed to spread out in all directions on the moon, where there should only be one source of light. Crosshairs on camera lenses are found to be behind objects, instead of in front of them. Deep footprints were produced by astronauts on the moon's dusty surface, which apparently has no moisture, and would, therefore, prevent footprints of that type from being created.

The American flag waves in the wind, on a satellite where no such wind should be found because the moon contains no asmosphere. There are also no stars in the sky in NASA's pictures, and the same exact background appears in films that supposedly portray separate locations on the moon.

Photographs also show what appear to be stage props and lighting cables on the moon's surface, and carefully directed film footage of landings of lunar modules seem to be taken by an external source already on the surface.

Additionally, a dust crater is not found underneath the lunar module, which the thrust of a powerful descent engine would have caused, nor are the LM's padded feet covered in dust after its landing.

Neil Armstrong has bravely tried to defend the moon landings as being factual, but has made a series of erroneous statements as a result. He tried to explain the American flag waving in the wind by saying that he drew "movement lines" on it with a pen. He also said that the moon smells of iron filings, despite such an aroma being impossible without an atmosphere to carry it. Moreover, how was Armstrong able to smell anything with a helmet on?

We should remember that Armstrong is an American patriot who would have believed that his part in a moon deception was best for his country at that time. We should also consider his fear of being assassinated for spilling the beans, a fate that has befallen a great deal of people who worked on the Apollo missions.

It is true that the moon has always been associated with lunacy and madness, but for the American government to have participated in such a stunt as faking moon landings seems incredible. Yet there is simply no good evidence to suggest that we ever went. I am not saying that we did not go to the moon. I'm saying the evidence presented by NASA suggests that we stayed on Earth.

There are also some other factors to take into consideration. If mankind can do something once, then it shall be done again and again. Once conquered, the extremes of physical location no longer become so extreme.

For instance, Mount Everest has been climbed repeatedly since Hillary and Tenzing reached its summit in 1953. Why then has it been 40 years since we visited the moon? Why do we not have a communications station, a military outpost, a scientific observatory and a hotel up there?

The answer may be simply that we can't build on the moon because we can't travel to the moon.

Perhaps we can land probes up there, but from the evidence it is doubtful humans can set foot on the moon as yet. Indeed, the reason why nobody in political power has suggested that we build something on the moon is because it would require the embarrassing situation of explaining that the Apollo missions were all staged and filmed in an aircraft hanger in Nevada. For politicians to tell us the truth of this matter really would be one giant leap for mankind, and a suicidal leap for NASA.

Another consideration is that Russia supposedly landed a remote controlled vehicle on the moon in November, 1970. This vehicle was called "Lunokhod 1," a solar powered buggy designed to beam back television pictures of the lunar surface. A triumph of technology, coming eleven years after Russia first sent an unmanned probe to the moon. So, why can we not see live pictures of the moon now? Why can't we drive the Lunokhod to the sites of any one of the six apparent Apollo landings and see the remains of the lunar modules for ourselves?

The Lunokhod consideration could, by itself, author the conspiracy theory that the Russians know and can prove that America has never gone to the moon and are being paid for their silence. Indeed, this could also be reason for China's new manned space exploration, to suggest that they have the technology to go to the moon, and instead receive a substantial bribe by the U.S. government not to do so.

To conclude the matter of conspiracy theories, if there really is a New World Order of Illuminati, be they Freemasons, vampires, reptiles or members of trans-global organisations of political leaders and businessmen such as the Bildeberg Group, then so what? Someone has to run the world.

And if JFK was shot by the CIA, Diana killed by MI6 and the TWA 800 shot down by the U.S. Navy, that's just too bad. At this stage in our evolution such matters are almost irrelevant. The masses are more concerned with how to pay their electricity bills, or how to feed their children. This is the reason why conspiracies can indeed exist, because people are simply too busy trying to make a living to care.

The average man on the street doesn't need or want the complications of conspiracy in his life; he wants food on the table and a holiday twice a year. As I said, most people think Lee Harvey Oswald did not kill JFK. Yet, aside from Oliver Stone, no one has made a fuss over the matter. Nobody really cares!

People who know the truth behind a conspiracy are generally in positions of power, or members of an elite social circle, so they certainly would not jeopardise their privileged positions by telling the truth. If, however, someone stumbles upon the truth by accident, and is keen to tell the world's media, "suicide" or a mysterious accident will quickly come their way.

We are all part of a conspiracy—the conspiracy of silence. If you are afraid of telling the police the whereabouts of a local drug dealer for fear of having your home burnt to the ground out of his revenge, why do you think people would not be afraid to tell the media about government conspiracies? Governments are infinitely more dangerous than a junkie with a disposable lighter.

The American intelligence community may be especially dangerous to civilian lives simply because it is not as competent as it would like to imagine. Does the CIA know everything, or is it stumbling in the dark like the rest of us?

The attacks of September 11th raised the question of whether the CIA knew of an impending attack and did nothing, or whether it was completely unaware of such vile plans, therefore negating its "intelligence" ability. Either answer is rather depressing.

Conspiracy theorists believe that the CIA did indeed know of the impending attacks on America, and submit some unusual facts to back their argument. Moreover, there are a growing number of people who believe 9/11 was actually planned by CIA boffins and the American government, to give the

U.S. an excuse to expand its already aggressive foreign policy regarding the Middle East.

Let's have a brief look at some of the details of this theory.

In 1994 "The Futurist" magazine published an article that highlighted the World Trade Center as an ideal target for terrorists who wanted to destroy a great symbol of both America and of global capitalism.

On September 7th, 2001, American citizens working overseas reported that they had been given a warning to be especially cautious by the U.S. State Department.

But what was there to be cautious about? The answer could have been found in the June 23rd issue of "Airjet Airline World News," which published a story concerning the possibility of an extreme security risk over the following weeks. This proves that there were certainly rumblings and rumours in the airline industry about an impending attack. Could the threat have been similar to the Algerian hijackers who were shot in 1994 as they tried to demand that an Air France jet head towards the Eiffel Tower?

In Russia, readers of "Pravda" may have been surprised to read on the morning of July 12th, 2001 that the U.S. economy was heading for disaster. An interior minister for economic development seemed to have heard that something was "more destructive, besides bombs and missiles." Could the minister have been referring to four commercial airliners?

Even if there had been knowledge of terrorist activity, and despite Osama Bin Laden's warning of attacks on the U.S. in 1997, where would the target be? Did anyone know? Perhaps someone could also explain why various members of a Bronx mosque were told to keep away from lower Manhattan on September 11th, several days before the tragic events unfolded, a directive that several New York Muslims later divulged to the FBI.

Did Flight 77 actually crash into the Pentagon? If so, why was there so little damage to the building? Where were the bodies of the dead passengers? Where was their luggage? Why did nobody see an airliner hit the building? Was the Pentagon actually hit by a missile or a remote controlled drone "Global Hawk" spy aircraft?

Why does video footage of the aircraft that crashed into the World Trade Center show an explosive flash before the planes actually connect with the twin towers? Why did firemen report hearing a series of explosions at the bottom of the towers? Why did Building 7 collapse so quickly, just because of a few fires? Were the twin towers and Building 7 actually "pulled" by controlled demolition experts and were not victims of fire? Was the demolition of the World Trade Center nothing more than a multi-billion dollar insurance scam?

Why did they find a passport belonging to one of the terrorists in the smoking ruins and rubble of the World Trade Center, yet they couldn't find any of the "black boxes" from Flights 11 and 175?

Did the passengers of doomed Flight 93 cry "let's roll" before they bravely tried to fight terrorists in an attempt to regain control of their plane? Or did the U.S. Air Force shoot them down in Pennsylvania? Did passengers on board Flight 93 make strangely worded calls to family and friends on mobile phones, despite it being virtually impossibly to do so given their high altitude? Did Flight 93 even exist? If so, where did all the dead passengers and the wreckage of the plane itself go? Only a large smoking hole was found at the scene of the apparent accident.

These are all questions as yet unanswered, but which give conspiracy theorists endless hours of amusement.

The most popular 9/11 conspiracy theories can be discovered in the documentary "Loose Change" and the book "Painful Questions," both of which draw some pretty disturbing conclusions surrounding the tragedy. Conclusions that, if true, throw a spanner in the works if you think the American government cares a damn for the American people.

After 9/11, America waged its "War on Terror," and invaded Afghanistan and Iraq, claiming these countries were the homeland bases of Osama Bin Laden and his secret army of Islamic terrorists. America and Britain concocted the myth of "weapons of mass destruction" as a further excuse to wage war, involving weapons that were never in fact found. Perhaps they disappeared and vanished into thin air along with elusive bogeyman Osama Bin Laden. Moreover, there is no evidence to show a link between Iraq and the late dictator Saddam Hussein with the attacks of 9/11, despite both the American government and media suggesting otherwise.

Whatever the truth of 9/11, whether it was the result of evil terrorist attacks or a CIA-planned American excuse to go to war with Iraq to steal its oil, many people have died as a result. Tens of thousands of both civilians and soldiers in America, Afghanistan and Iraq have lost their lives and the death toll continues to rise. Civil unrest and division between rival Muslim factions in Iraq continued for years, and Iraq became America's new "Vietnam."

Furthermore, strange video clips of Muslim fanatics kept being aired on TV to perpetuate the idea that Americans were under constant threat from Muslim terrorists, and to enable the government to remove more and more of their Constitutional rights, apparently for their own protection. These clips perpetuated the Muslim threat and kept money flowing into the American war machine.

Curiously, some video clips of Osama Bin Laden threatening the West did not really resemble Bin Laden at all. Nor did video clips of white American-Muslim converts making the same threats of violence and war against infidels seem credible. What Islamic terrorist organisation would welcome a white American convert into their fold? They would surely think he was working for the CIA, and they would be correct. Of course, white Muslim converts who make threatening videos aired on TV are working for the CIA, too. But instead of their videos being filmed in the tent of an Al Qaeda terrorist camp, they are more likely to have been filmed in a back room at CIA headquarters in Langley, Virginia.

Here is one more consideration. If you are looking for someone to blame, and don't think Islamic terrorists were skilled enough to fly hijacked planes in the manner described by the official 9/11 report, or that the CIA would be so callous as to plan the death of American citizens, who else could be guilty? Aliens? Shape shifting reptilian Illuminati? Or maybe even a secret criminal network similar to James Bond's enemies, "SPECTRE"?

I think it is interesting that the Jewish landlords of the World Trade Center made over $7 billion dollars in insurance claims after 9/11. I'm just saying that it's fascinating that Israel's Prime Minister cancelled a trip to New York just prior to the day of the attacks. And I'm only suggesting that just maybe Israel's secret service ("Mossad") may have been the true architects of 9/11. Perhaps 9/11 was planned as an attempt to get America and Britain to retaliate against Israel's Muslim enemies in the Middle East, something beyond an attack on the World Trade Center and Pentagon alone.

One final possibility—there could be a round table in a secret room in a hidden castle somewhere in a forgotten land that has three places set for dinner. Three greedy friends will dine on the flesh of men. The first guest will eat halal flesh, the second guest will gorge on kosher flesh, leaving a cheeseburger of flesh and a slice of Mom's apple pie for guest number three. Rich Muslims, rich Jews and rich Christian Americans may simply be playing with the rest of us. Perhaps we are merely pawns in their global game of chess. Perhaps the only enemies of freedom and the peoples of the world are the handful of billionaire tyrants who run the planet. Perhaps, to these tyrants, the division of religion and nationality does not exist. Perhaps the only division is between those who have money, privilege and power, and those who do not.

All of this is food for thought.

The other side of conspiracy theories to consider, other than sending shivers up our spine, is that any theory, no matter how bizarre, can be concocted using available evidence.

For example, on October 30, 2001 newspaper reports detailed a car crash that brought memories flooding back to Beatles fans of when Paul McCartney had safely walked away from a car crash in Long Island. This time he had not been "killed!" In late 1969, only months before the Beatles were to disband, the situation was quite the reverse. Stories of McCartney's "death" eventually led the angry pop star to throw a bucket of water over some of the reporters who installed themselves on the gates of his Scottish farm. Such an action was surely not the behavior of a real Beatle, the darling of royalty and idol to millions.

Alerted by the reports of McCartney's death, Beatle-maniacs around the globe began to piece together a bizarre patchwork of "facts" that proved without a shadow of a doubt that the Fab Four had actually been the Fab Three for many years. Moreover, it was thought that both Paul and the details of his untimely death had been buried by the powers that be, and the pop legend had been replaced by a look-alike.

Backed up by Beatles song lyrics and LP artwork, the story goes that Paul McCartney was killed circa 1965, at the age of 23, the day after "Yesterday" had reached number 1 in the US charts. Seeing their chance to make a breakthrough to the global marketplace at last, the British music industry had simply silenced reports of Paul's death. The British establishment also played its part in the conspiracy, giving the pop band MBEs in an attempt to woo the nations' rebellious youth back into the fold of conformity. News of McCartney's death would certainly have torpedoed this ambition more quickly than a yellow submarine chased by a giant glove.

It was supposed that Paul had picked up a female hitchhiker in his white sports car at 5:00 a.m. on the morning of Wednesday October. Being under the influence of both alcohol and drugs, and distracted by the girl in question, McCartney took his eyes off the road and crashed into an oncoming vehicle. The impostor who took McCartney's place is rumoured to have been, and still is, a Scottish/Canadian gentleman named William Campbell, a man who can be seen in the *Magical Mystery Tour* book dressed as an army major, sitting behind a sign boasting "I You Was."

Also in the book is Paul's double holding a funeral bouquet of flowers, whilst wearing a black carnation in his lapel. The other three Beatles have a red carnation. In other *Magical Mystery Tour* pictures the late George Harrison is discovered sitting in the middle of a road, about to be knocked down by a white sports car, whilst Ringo is found with "Love 3 Beatles" printed on his drum kit.

Other albums, such as "Sergeant Pepper's" and "Abbey Road," seem to provide a plethora of both morbid lyrics and sinister artwork, all suggesting Paul's unfortunate death. This evidence indeed points to something suspicious, but perhaps nothing more bizarre than John Lennon's weird sense of humour. After all, there is nothing better than a death conspiracy to boost record sales.

However, perhaps the only way of knowing whether or nor Paul was killed in 1965 is by asking his girlfriend at the time, Jane Asher. After all, William Campbell's face may have had a striking resemblance to Paul, but what about the rest of his body? Perhaps McCartney would himself say that he was an impostor, as a way of excusing the dire musical ventures of Wings.

In conclusion, conspiracy theories can hang on the thinnest thread of "evidence," or perhaps seem so disturbing and depressing that we simply don't want to consider the possibility that they are true. But fact is often stranger than fiction, and I suggest that you consider all possibilities, no matter how absurd they seem. At least that way you won't die of shock when they confess that President George W. Bush was not human, but a brainless and remote controlled automaton whose every movement was dictated by a group of juvenile reptilian Illuminati.

The Media

"Don't believe everything you read in the papers," people will often say. Yet they may well be the same people who do indeed believe what they read in the papers. Similar to politicians, we are always prepared to give newspaper reports the benefit of the doubt. Whilst there are obvious deceptions, such as stories of World War II bombers being found on the moon, as reported by a British pornographic tabloid, other stories that contain few facts are not quite so easy to detect.

Tabloid newspapers are especially guilty of inventing "facts" to tie in with their partially informed stories, facts that usually sprinkle a glittering layer of sleaze on someone's portfolio.

Sleaze sells newspapers. Although most editors and journalists who work for tabloids are from middle-class, highly educated backgrounds, they all pander to the lowest common denominator in society. Whilst a daily polemic on relative ethics won't attract the money or attention of the masses, a picture of a naked woman and an exposé of a pervert priest certainly will.

Yet the widespread "dumbing-down" process is not entirely the fault of cynical editors; we are all guilty of gossip mongering. Always hoping someone else in the world is just as devious as us, we seek his or her stories in the tabloids and hypocritically condemn such misbehaviour.

We then convince ourselves that we are not quite as bad as the person whom we are reading about. As we no longer live in medieval hamlets where good old gossip about the village idiot or harlot was routine, we now collect the same kind of gossip from "Red-Tops." Moreover, the ubiquitous interest in soap operas and celebrity lives also provides us with a wealth of such trashy, meaningless gossip, hence why newspapers fill their pages with this rubbish.

Aside from the shallow world of tabloid journalism, there is a more sinister aspect of newspaper, radio, television and Internet reporting of the news. So-called "hard news" can be reported by serious journalists, and presented in such a manner as to be slightly short of the whole truth.

If a broad-sheet journalist wears an expensive suit, talks with a posh accent and doesn't rely on smutty double entendres to articulate a point, it does not mean we can trust what he says any more than a corrupt hack scribbling for a local rag. Furthermore, if a news medium has strong ties with government or business institutions, there is a great risk of their reports being skewed and out of focus.

Remember, most news media are businesses like any other, who do not wish to alienate themselves from their peers or important contacts. Therefore, the final product, which we understand as being the news, is edited to consider the position of advertisers, valuable sources, the threat of legal action, and the ideological and political viewpoint of the owner company or individual.

For example, the British media displayed old imperial ties to Australia when it reported on a ship full of illegal immigrants heading towards antipodean shores. Although the Canberra government may well have been correct in its decision not to allow the immigrants sanctuary, pro-Australian British news reports did not consider the immigrants alternative position in detail. Moreover, when the Pacific Republic of Nauru offered to accommodate the immigrants on their island, it seemed to bring an end to the matter.

However, what was not reported is that living on Nauru offers nothing more to unwelcome immigrants than virtual imprisonment, with no hope of future success. This is due to the fact that Nauruan landowners have become exceedingly wealthy by selling phosphates quarried out of the island on a vast scale. Such quarrying has resulted in a virtual lunar landscape being created, which will eventually force Nauru's inhabitants to live elsewhere.

So not only have a ship load of illegal immigrants found themselves on an island where all food, clothing and resources are imported at great cost, but they may also be marooned on an uninhabitable wasteland. When this happens, perhaps the illegal immigrants will be the subject of news reports once again, their story being a miserable warning to other such refugees about the fate of those who illegally sail to Australia.

The deception connected with the media is the belief that it is reliable, fair, unbiased and objective. Yet the truth remains that news organisations are owned by the same companies who make vast profits from entertainment, sports, and publishing. Therefore, the captive animal known as news media cannot kill its capitalist master, lest it starve to death.

For example, media mogul Rupert Murdoch chairs a multinational corporation that owns nearly two hundred newspapers around the world, including The New York Post, The Times and The Sun. The same company owns Fox and Sky TV, Harper Collins books, and sponsors the Australian national rugby team. Whilst Time-Warner, the owner of Warner Bros films, also controls AOL, CNN, Time Magazine, 24 book publishers, 52 record labels and the rights to the Harry Potter brand.

Thus the news reported on a daily basis is filled with inane stories about the lives of celebrities and petty criminals, and not of the international businessmen who get away with large-scale crime and corruption. This phenomenon occurs simply because the businessmen who get away with large-scale crime and corruption own the world's media, and possibly governments and lawmakers to boot.

Entertainment

Ever since our prehistoric days as troglodytes, humans have employed deception in all manner of ways to entertain family members and companions. Acting and the wearing of costumes gave people the opportunity to mimic someone or something else, either for the purpose of comedy, tragedy, or social and political satire. In the western world, such entertainment was to become formalised drama by Athenian decree in 488 B.C.E., eventually to blossom into the glittering entity known as "show business."

Essentially the aim of show business is to cheer us up a bit, or to make us ponder over a writer's social comment, as performed by actors, puppets, animations, etc. However, in order that we can be successfully entertained we have to suspend our disbelief in the entertainer's environment or situation. We have to allow ourselves to be temporarily deceived. We have to imagine that an actor's costume, make-up or mask is the genuine garb and appearance of an actual being, not someone just pretending. Moreover, as an actor, one has to deceive one's conscious self into believing that we are indeed the character we are trying to portray, in order that we may bring some authenticity to the role.

Yet even before we have set foot inside the door of a theatre, we may have been deceived, especially if an emboldened quote or review of a certain play has been plastered on a billboard outside. "This show is the greatest" a promotional poster may boast, perhaps even accompanied by the name of the quote's source, a newspaper or critic, for example. However, what the public has to remember is that the generous quote may have been the only good thing to come out of a myriad of newspapers, whose reviewers all hated the show. Moreover, the published quote in question may have been extracted from a longer statement, such as "This show is the greatest pile of rubbish I have ever seen."

Apart from the process of acting, the technical aspects of stagecraft require a vast catalogue of deception. In the theatre, stage sets, Tromp-l'Oile back-cloths, and properties (props) can be made to look like rooms, houses, streets or any everyday object, but are often no more than hollow papier-mâché or canvas representations. The illusion given by a set, of an actual place or object, is often so realistic that those who work on stage often find themselves on the cusp of that which is genuine and that which is a deception.

Special effects such as strobe lighting can also be employed in the theatre to help an audience believe they are witnessing a spectacular event, but such effects do not end at the stage door. Radio, television and film technicians also use light and sound effects, complicated pyrotechnics and computer generated images to facilitate the process of deception.

Indeed, there is so much computer-aided deception in modern cinema and television that it is now possible to represent anyone, at any place, doing any thing, which is a situation that presents television and film producers with a powerful tool with which to entertain us or con us. Whilst most of us would like to imagine that such images of fraud and fakery would be obvious, such as Elvis being crowned pope, how many of us still believe we actually saw astronauts land on the moon?

It is possible that the best example of deception used as a method of entertainment is found in stage magic and illusion. Using tricks such as pulling a rabbit out of a hat or making a tank disappear, magicians have been using clever trickery to make us gasp and cheer for countless millennia. Whether it be Moses turning his staff into a snake, Jesus turning water into wine, Merlin procuring a sword from a water nymph or Houdini denying himself oxygen for half an hour, humans never cease to be amazed, fooled and baffled by such actions.

It is not surprising that we are fooled by stage magic, being that so much thought and effort has gone into the invention of a magician's tricks—tricks that may have been devised thousands of years ago. Moreover, if such trickery is complimented by a dramatic build-up, costumes and effects, all presented in a slightly eerie environment, we are more likely to confuse illusion with reality.

Whilst modern stage magicians have used glamorous young assistants to distract the attention of an audience as they quickly hide a card up their sleeve, street magicians use their environment to bring a sense of reality to their tricks. To them, the street is regarded as belonging to all, and cannot be commonly manipulated by a wandering entertainer.

For example, a modern street illusionist such as David Blaine may pick up the tiny corpse of a dead fly from a shop's dusty window sill, before magically bringing the insect back to life. Such an illusion would no doubt send shivers up the collective spine of his quickly assembled audience, who would all have convinced themselves that it could not possibly be a trick. How did he bring the fly back to life? How could he know there would be a fly there in the first place? We don't know the answer, so it must be real! Praise Allah, it's a miracle.

The answer is that, prior to the show, the magician placed the fly in a small net atop a container of liquid nitrogen, or dry ice. Faced with such low temperatures, most insects will slow down their body's metabolism to ensure their survival throughout a harsh winter, essentially hibernating until the warmth of the sun returns. The magician put the fly on the window sill a few moments before he assembled a crowd together, and then simply warmed the poor wee insect up in his hands, eventually allowing it to fly off to freedom.

Therefore, the magician's trick was an example of how a good understanding of science can aid the art of dramatic deception.

In card tricks, not only is hand and eye coordination a must with regard to misdirecting the intrusive glare of a sceptical audience, but an understanding of math is also a bonus.

The great vaudeville entertainer and magician, Si Stebbins, created a range of mathematical card tricks that baffled American audiences for a period of nearly forty years. However, his most famous card trick was quite simple in its conception. His deck was merely arranged in a way that looked completely random, but which actually followed a set pattern and used a mnemonic code-breaker.

Essentially the deck was arranged in a sequence that produced a value of three or more than the value of the previous card. The sequence was also arranged in four stacks, when the cards were being assembled, so that each stack began with a 3 and ended with a King. The cards were placed by suits as well as values, all following the repeating pattern of Clubs, Hearts, Spades, Diamonds, Clubs and so on. Therefore, when a card was picked from the assembled deck, all Stebbins would have to remember was that the cards ascended by threes, i.e. 3, 6, 9, Q, 2, 5, 8, J, A, 4, 7, 10, K, and that the card suits were represented by the secret word: "CHaSeD."

The trick would, therefore, be Stebbins asking the audience not to tell him what card had been chosen, whilst he'd simply have a quick glance at the card prior to the one now missing. If he caught sight of the 2 of Clubs he knew it was the 5 of Hearts that had been picked. If the 3 of Spades remained, the 6 of Diamonds was missing; clever and simple, yet a very effective trick. A Stebbins audience was always convinced that he could actually read minds—a lovely deception.

It is quite often the case that the simplest deceptions are the most effective, most believable, and most rewarding for those who employ them. The three matchbox trick, for example, is a piece of "magic" that anyone can master, but which can fool even the most sceptical of observers.

Essentially the trick involves three matchboxes, one of which is half full of matches. The boxes are placed on a table and one is shown to have matches inside. As observers watch the magician mix up the order of the boxes, he pauses to shake one of the boxes, which rattles with the sound of matches. He then makes a deliberate mess of jumbling them up so as the observers can successfully follow the box that he rattled. The magician then asks one of the observers to point to the box with matches in it. Unfortunately the box, when examined, will be empty.

The trick was that that the magician had a fourth box of matches up his sleeve, which ratted when he shook the empty one from the table. Although this trick can be used to entertain family members at a Christmas party, it can also be used to remove money from gullible fools, if betting on the matchboxes is encouraged. Therefore, never bet on anything that comes in threes, be they cards, walnut shells or matchboxes.

Another type of magic, the "magic" of television and cinema, has today taken illusion and special effects into a new realm, where the imagination of writers and directors can become an unlimited reality. Advances in computer and digital technology have thus made it possible for film makers to create everything from alien landscapes on a distant planet to squadrons of World War I aircraft in the midst of a raging dogfight.

However, the use of computer graphics can also create the possibility of reproducing the image and voice of almost any human being, be they alive or dead. Deceased actors can now star in humorous adverts for cars or chocolates, or perhaps entire feature length films.

However, there is also a darker side to this technology. Not only will it be possible to frame someone, by producing a film of them robbing a bank or committing a murder, but living actors may no longer be required to show up at a studio in person, just give permission for their image to be recreated.

For example, an actor who has great box office pulling power, but who is also notorious for there tantrums and spoiled behaviour, may be better directed if, in fact, they only existed in a computer's memory. How the public will react to this deception, only time will tell, but if films and pop videos could be made quite legitimately without having to worry about upsetting the star by forgetting to remove all the brown M&Ms from the sweet bowl, how happy directors and technical crews would be.

In the music industry, audio deception can make people who can't sing to save their lives sound as if they have powerful voices, albeit with plenty of amplification, overdubbing and editing. In 1990 it was revealed that the pop duo "Milli Vanilli" did not even sing on their album. Record producer Frank Farian, who had himself manufactured the male voice of "Boney-M," had been named as the trickster behind the fraud. His deception was seen to be especially embarrassing for the music industry in general when Milli Vanilli was awarded a Grammy for the group's work, an award they handed back before stumbling into a fatal world of alcohol and drug abuse.

Thus it could even be argued that the pop industry has today become more concerned with image than sound, an anathema to the concept of music. Dance combos who claim to be "bands" happily prance around in a state of near undress, whilst miming to a vaguely musical track played in the background. It is not quality music, but it seems to amuse the 8 to 12 year-old children who purchase such abominable wares.

When we look at the world of entertainment and literature we find many movies, plays, TV shows, books and music acts that seem to be so similar to something else we have seen, read or heard that we may correctly assume that intellectual and artistic theft is commonplace.

Are writers, actors, directors and musicians simply producing their wares to be a respectful homage to something that has gone before, or are they ripping off someone else's ideas? Are they being heavily influenced by the original creation and simply updating and improving it, or are they totally lacking in originality?

Your favourite boy band may seem original to you, or your six-year-old daughter, but have they copied their romantic songs and fun-loving image from The Monkeys, a sixties pop foursome consisting of actors playing the part of musicians for a TV show, and eventually actual music concerts, who in turn manufactured their entire look to resemble the early Beatles?

Or maybe your favourite band is a heavy metal or hard rock act. Maybe you think the latest shocking thrash metal combo is original, when actually anything shocking in the world of metal and hard rock has been done by the likes of Black Sabbath, Alice Cooper, The Who and The Rolling Stones, all of whom have copied to some degree the outrageous bad behaviour of rock and roll legends such as Jerry Lee Lewis, Little Richard and Chuck Berry, or the Halloween horror mask antics of showmen such as Screamin' Jay Hawkins and Screaming Lord Sutch.

Maybe you imagine the blood splattered satanic image of Marilyn Manson or Rob Zombie to be an indication of their devotion to the dark arts, a brave new statement in the world or rock. In actuality it is Black Sabbath, Alice Cooper and Led Zeppelin who should take the credit for being the bands with a stronger link to the occult, Led Zeppelin having Jimmy Page, guitar guru and Aleister Crowley expert, as the founding member. Page was a talented musician of amazing ability who has been criticised for "borrowing" most of his guitar riffs from bluesmen such as Buddy Guy, Robert Johnson, Albert King and Willie Dixon. Led Zeppelin itself was also shamelessly mimicked by bands such as Blind Melon, Wolfmother, Def Leppard, Deep Purple and Whitesnake.

The similarities between different TV shows, films and books are often so close that we should ask ourselves whether some writers have either forgotten about the existence of a strikingly familiar film or story, or are actually committing artistic theft and plagiarism.

It might be said that the horror themed sitcom "The Addams Family" was a copy of "The Munsters." Furthermore, it could be said that both Lily Munster and Morticia Addams were both inspired by "The Bride of Frankenstein," the "New Yorker" cartoons of Charles Addams and TV hostess "Vampira," Vampira herself inspiring the later incarnation of "Elvira," MTV's "mistress of the dark."

It could be argued that the movie "Battlestar Galactica" was a sad and shoddy Star Wars rip-off, or that "Independence Day" was a clone of "War of the Worlds" and the TV mini-series "V." It could be said that "Mr Ed," "Champion the Wonder Horse," "Flipper," "Skippy," "The Littlest Hobo" and "Lassie Come Home" were all influenced by the Edgar Rice Burroughs novel "Tarzan," concerning the close links mankind has with remarkably intelligent animals. Tarzan is a copy of Rudyard Kipling's "Jungle Book," which itself is a kissing cousin of the Hindu myths and legends of India, and indeed of any world mythology and fables concerning anthropomorphic beasts.

If you like westerns with cowboys chasing savage Indians, a concept that is a deception itself, as the cowboys should be the ones labelled as savages, you may think there are only three or four stories at most that can be told about the subject. Most cowboy films look almost identical to each other, especially if they star John "The Duke" Wayne, a tough guy (real name, Marion Morrison) whose own deception was that he played patriotic American heroes in countless war epics, and yet refused to enlist in the armed forces during WWII.

As a fan of westerns you may also note the embarrassing similarities with your favourite cowboy movies and the cinematic products of the Hong Kong martial arts genre. Comparisons can be made between westerns and essentially anything Bollywood has ever made—Bollywood being the collective name of India's film industry, which creates an extensive catalogue of Hollywood clones for the Asian market. For example, if you liked the 1991 movie "A Kiss Before Dying," starring Matt Dillon, itself a remake of a 1956 movie starring Robert Wagner, then you would like the Bollywood recreation, "Baazigar," starring Shahrukh Khan. The only difference is that in the Bollywood clone the obligatory dance scenes and songs are present.

Of all the copies and clones in the world of literature, the most shocking and notorious example of plagiarism is apparently (I have to say "apparently" to avoid being sued) is J.K. Rowling's "creation," "Harry Potter."

J.K. Rowling (real name, Jo Murray) the thirteenth richest woman in Britain, is a writer who has sold more than 400 million books worldwide, and who has earned around £545 million pounds for doing so. However, anyone who has read a *Harry Potter* book or watched a *Harry Potter* movie may possibly have a strong sense of déjà vu and a feeling that something is very familiar. Especially if they are a fantasy fiction book or "Star Wars" movie fan. Whilst the "sorcerer's apprentice" is a popular character in children's literature, plots from the original "Star Wars" movies are also seemingly mimicked. Even the Harry Potter theme tune is reminiscent of "Star Wars" in parts.

In the *Harry Potter* series a boy who makes rebellious friends, travels to a secret land to learn the ways of a wizard, and uses magic to fight a dark lord who killed his parents, often with his flashing wand, under the tutelage of a wise and powerful teacher. In the *Star Wars* series, a young man who makes friends with rebels travels to a secret planet to learn the ways of a Jedi, and uses "the Force" to fight a dark lord who killed his parents (he assumes), often with his flashing light sabre, under the tutelage of a wise and powerful teacher. If you replace mythological beasts with aliens, castles with space-ships, flying brooms with hover speeders, and black magic with the dark side of "the Force," *Harry Potter* and *Star Wars* begin to look quite similar."

Essentially, the *Harry Potter* series is the story of a young orphan boy who lives with cruel step-parents, in the real world, and who attends a school of magic, in a fantasy world, to become a wizard. Potter is popular with children and adults alike, despite the criticism that the books are neither intellectually challenging, well written, nor are they original (apparently).

J.K. Rowling has explained that she got the idea for "Harry Potter" whilst sitting on a train to King's Cross in London, and that she then spent months sitting in cafes writing her first and subsequent books based on the magical adventures of the lovable character. However, critics of this story have suggested that perhaps Rowling spent months sitting in front of the TV, during her time as an unemployed English language teacher—for most of what she has written can apparently be traced to TV shows, movies, or earlier books and stories, not least of which is the work of J.R.R. Tolkien (*Lord of the Rings*) and C.S. Lewis (*The Lion, The Witch and The Wardrobe*).

For example, *The Worst Witch*, written by Jill Murphy in 1974, details the story of Mildred Hubble, a trainee witch at Miss Cackle's Academy of Witchcraft. The occult adventures of Mildred Hubble were transferred to TV in the 1980s and produced a show that many people have said looked exactly like the "Harry Potter" movies, just without the expensive special effects and monsters.

Then there was Sabrina the Teenage Witch, originally a character contained in "Archie's Madhouse" comics from 1962 onwards, inspired by the movie "Bell, Book and Candle," itself a rip-off of the 1942 movie "I Married a Witch," which inspired the TV show "Bewitched." Sabrina moved to TV in 1996, one year before "Harry Potter" was published, which, many have said, would make it impossible to be a source of inspiration for *Harry Potter* the book, as the writing and publishing process takes much longer than a year. However, the Sabrina comic books remain! As do the TV shows and movies "Bewitched," "Mr. Merlin," "Dragonslayer," "The Sorcerer's Apprentice," "Krull" and "Hawk the Slayer," all of which cover the idea of learning magic or wizardry, or fighting it.

"Hawk the Slayer" should be pointed out as being either a rip-off or a tongue in cheek homage to Clint Eastwood's spaghetti westerns, "Star Wars" and "The Magnificent Seven," the latter film being a copy and remake of "The Seven Samurai."

Then there's the fantasy fiction catalogue of books by Ian Livingstone and Steve Jackson throughout the seventies and eighties, and their other "Dungeons and Dragons" gaming publications such as *White Dwarf* and *The Warlock of Firetop Mountain*. The entire genre of fantasy fiction masterminded by these two authors covers anything in the "Harry Potter" books. And let's not forget Terry Pratchett's *Discworld* series of fantasy fiction books beginning in 1983.

It could be argued that if you assembled the entire collection of Livingstone, Jackson and Pratchett books, tore out every tenth page, and stapled the torn out pages together, you'd have the basic plot and scene structure of a "Harry Potter" novel. The word "novel," however, implies originality, so I prefer to say "book."

Then there's Diana Wynne, who wrote *Charmed Life* in 1977, concerning orphans learning magic in a castle. Sound familiar?

There's also Ursula K. Le Guin, who wrote *A Wizard of Earthsea* in 1968, about a boy who learns magic in a school for wizards, who discovers his true identity and who fights a sinister monster. Sound familiar? Le Guin may have given, without consent, her middle initial "K" to Rowling.

It could be argued that Rowling may also have borrowed the names "Harry Potter" and "Muggles" from American author Nancy K. Stouffer, who wrote *Larry Potter* and *The Legend of Rah and the Muggles*. Rowling may also have borrowed the initial "K" from Stouffer.

In 2002 Stouffer tried unsuccessfully to sue Rowling for plagiarism and stealing her ideas, but her case was destroyed by Rowling's powerful legal team who suggested Stouffer had manipulated the publication dates, artwork and sales numbers of her books to support her copyright infringement action. After her court battle, Stouffer received constant death threats from Harry Potter fans, which continue to this day.

If Rowling did not lift the name "Harry Potter" and the artwork of a boy with glasses from Stouffer, some people have pointed out that in the 1986 horror movie "Troll," a young boy who enters a magical domain is called "Harry Potter, Jr." However, Harry Potter is just a name and may well be shared by hundreds of people around the planet. Yet the controversy surrounding the now famous name shows that "Harry Potter" should not legally belong to either Rowling or Warner Brothers, who call a lawyer whenever the name is mentioned. In the same way, the McDonalds hamburger chain should not be able to sue a person called "McDonald" if they open up a hamburger restaurant.

Then there's Neil Gaiman, who wrote *The Books of Magic* in 1989, about a boy with glasses and a pet owl, who thinks his destiny is to be the world's best wizard. Sound familiar?

Yet another example is Jane Yolen, who wrote *Wizard's Hall* in 1991, about a boy called Henry who learns magic in a school for wizards, and who must fulfil a prophecy to defeat a powerful and evil wizard. Sound familiar?

Consider that "Harry Potter," the global brand, is worth around $15 billion dollars, and that Rowling (a rich and loved author), Bloomsbury (a respected book publisher) and Warner Brothers (media giant and movie producer/distributor), a powerful trio indeed, share the brand. It is, therefore,

unlikely that any of the aforementioned authors will sue Rowling successfully for plagiarism, and those who indeed have a strong case to do so could
well be kept silent by a Warner Brothers bribe, if such a thing could ever happen. If so, would it come in the form of a 'buyout?"

Warner now apparently owns the rights to "Sabrina," *The Worst Witch* and
some of Neil Gaiman's work. We don't need a wise magical owl or a trip
through a secret doorway on a train platform to see why, do we?

As for Rowling's defense of her own intellectual property, if there is any,
both she and Warner Brothers come down hard on anyone who writes something even vaguely similar to Harry Potter, or which contains references to
the character.

For example, information on an internet web site run by Harry Potter fans
titled "The Harry Potter Lexicon" was to be converted to book format by
RDR Books, without Rowling's consent. However, Warner Brothers let their
legal war dogs loose on the small publisher and seem to have halted the venture. Rowling has said that she had the idea first, and that she is writing a
Harry Potter Encyclopedia. The irony of this case is that there could be little
in the Harry Potter lexicon that is truly the intellectual property of Rowling
to begin with.

Rowling did not invent most of the names she uses; "Harry," "Potter,"
"Hog," "Warts," "Magic," "Wizard" are all nouns that have been used for
many centuries in the English language. Nor is the idea of a boy who goes to
wizard school her intellectual property; magic potions, done before Rowling;
names of monsters, done before Rowling; anatomy of a castle, done before
Rowling. What exactly is it in the Harry Potter Lexicon or Encyclopedia that
Rowling and Warner Brothers imagine that they truly own?

Of course one of my own critics may ask me why I'm making such a fuss
about unoriginality. What is original? This very book of mine is not original.
The exposé of deception is as old as deception itself. Moreover, most of the
ideas within these page are not my own, I have simply collected them, summarised them and commented on them. Perhaps there was no "originality"
after *The Epic of Gilgamesh*, The Bible and the works of Homer. However,
that is not to say that blatantly copying someone's work should be acceptable, or that when an ungracious author takes the credit for something as old
as the hills we should keep silent. In the world of literature, imitation is nei-

ther sincere nor flattering. Plagiarism is an indication of desperation and that a lazy, uninspired and unimaginative writer has run out of ideas, not something that should lead to a bestseller!

Having said that, I'm thinking of writing a book about a boy who goes to wizard school to learn magic.

If you think I'm being unfair to Ms. Rowling, let me add that I think Harry Potter has aided parents and teachers all over the world in getting children to read books. Moreover, I think Rowling has charged a fair price for her books and has made her fortune in a perfectly acceptable manner with regard to selling her books at an affordable price.

But as for other rich and famous people of note, I don't agree with the ludicrously high salary that movie actors and celebrity sports stars are awarded. Thus a final deception in the world of entertainment is that actors and sports stars are worth what they are paid.

Let's, for instance, take Tom Cruise and David Beckham. One is screen actor and scientology fanatic, the other is a British soccer ace, male model, and has one of the world's most instantly recognizable faces. This is due to the fact that his face has been on posters in every major city on Earth, advertising everything from sunglasses and mobile phones, to soft drink and shoes.

Both are very talented men, they are great at what they do, and they deserve to be richer than the rest of us, right? Wrong!

How can an actor or a soccer player justify making a hundred times more money in a week than a doctor, fireman, electrician or hairdresser makes in a year? Cruise and Beckham entertain us, certainly, and what they do directly or indirectly generates income for a multitude of different industries that employ hundreds of thousands of people around the globe.

Moreover, with high calibre stars like Cruise and Beckham success is guaranteed, right? Wrong! Some of Tom Cruise's movies are flops at the box office and don't attract a large paying audience of moviegoers, whilst Beckham often fails to score a single goal in many games. So why pay them for something they fail to do?

If a doctor failed to cure you from a disease, you may die. If a fireman failed to drag you from a towering inferno, you may die. If an electrician failed to attach an earth wire to a washing machine he was fixing, your smelly socks may not be as shocking as the surprise you'd get when you tried to wash them. And if your wife or girlfriend has her black hair turned white by an incompetent hairdresser, who mistook a bleaching agent for shampoo, she may want to die or perhaps just "dye" when she looks in the mirror.

Ask yourself which is more important, watching a movie and a game of soccer, or keeping your health, being saved from a burning building, have electrical appliances that won't kill you, and getting an attractive hairstyle? What service is more valuable and for which would you pay good money? Would you trust the scientology of Mr. Cruise to save you from a nasty dose of the flu? Would you trust the football skills of Mr. Beckham to save you from a fire?

In this case, we can see that the people who have the least amount of practical skills earn far more than those who can save lives—the highest skill that humans possess. Why then do we judge people on their salary? A rich man is assumed to be worth more as a human being than a poor man, who is judged to be a worthless burden on society.

The low-paid man who takes the garbage away is more valuable to me than someone who kicks a ball around a grassy field, or who pretends to be a racing car driver or Air Force pilot. I mean, Cruise got paid a fortune for simply pretending to fly planes in "Top Gun," yet a real fighter pilot may only dream of earning a fraction of Cruise's salary in his whole career.

And what about paying someone based on their ability to succeed in what they do, every time they do it? David Beckham has made millions from simply being present on a soccer field. Regardless of whether or not he scores a goal, he will still go home with more money than most people on the planet will earn in a lifetime.

So we pay the least skilled the most money and for not doing what they are paid to do!

If an airline pilot had the same success rate as David Beckham, what would happen? Let's say Beckham scores a goal in only 60% of all the soccer matches in which he plays, and a pilot successfully flies and lands a jumbo jet 99% of the time. For Beckham's 40% failure rate he still gets paid and is called a hero, for the pilot's 1% failure to do his job he could cause the deaths of hundreds. If the same pilot were to fail to safely land a plane 40% of the time, he could bankrupt an airline and destroy the lives of many— crash victims and families of the deceased alike.

I say again, don't be deceived. Money is not a good indicator of a person's worth or the value of their skills. Having money simply means that a person is lucky enough to afford nice clothes and a decent car. A rich man is no more "valuable" than a poor man, he just has more money.

But this is not the *Communist Manifesto*, which wants no one to be rich. And I suppose if we were all multi-millionaires then nobody would take out the trash.

Sports and Games

Here are some sporting heroes to remember; jockey Kieren Fallon, body-builder Jesse Marunde, and sprinters Ben Johnson and Marion Jones. These men and women were very successful in their chosen sports, but what links them all? They were all accused of being cheats!

Kieren Fallon was a six-time champion horse racing jockey who, with two other jockeys, was in 2007 accused of "fixing" around 27 races. Fallon and his fellow conspirators were apparently paid to lose, simply by slowing their horses down. Such a thing could perhaps be the simplest con in the world of sports. Fallon was later cleared of the charges, with many questions still unanswered and a community of racetrack punters left unsure of who to trust. The next time they place a bet on the "favourite" horse to win a race, are they simply giving their money away to Asian business cartels who manipulate and control the outcomes of major races and prominent sports figures?

Canadian Ben Johnson was a very successful sprinter who won two Olympic bronze medals and one gold medal. He also set two world records for running the fastest 100m in 1987 and 1988. But was banished from athletics when he was found to have taken performance enhancing drugs and steroids.

Sydney Olympics heroine Marion Jones was a winner of three gold medals and two bronze medals, and had signed contracts for multimillion-dollar sponsorships and advertising deals when she was found guilty in 2007 of taking steroids and performance enhancing drugs.

Meanwhile, the 2005 second place winner of the "World's Strongest Man" contest died of a heart attack in 2007. Steroids were blamed for the 27 year-old man's untimely death. Although unproven, steroids may also have been responsible for the masculine and very muscular female sprinter "Flo-Jo" Griffith, who set world records for running the 100m and 200m.

Not only did it see the downfall of athletics and racing heroes, the year 2007 was also a bad year for football (soccer) as clubs throughout Italy and the U.K. were investigated for corruption. Several international players were accused of taking bribes to alter the outcome of a match.

Whether it be slowing down a horse on the racetrack, the illegal use of steroids in athletics and body building, or the use of marked cards and loaded dice, sport and games continue to produce a treasure trove of deception.

Generally speaking, games (rather than physical sports) involving two or more people are those intellectual activities that often rely on the skill of out-witting an opponent and bluffing your way past their mental guard. Sports, on the other hand, usually rely more on a physical talent, and an ability to outmatch an opponent's strength, speed or stamina.

In chess it is tactics that are matched, whereas in poker it is a player's use of deceptive throw-downs and facial expressions which will often win him the round, rather than having a Royal Flush or three of a kind. Facial twitch-es and frowns, known as "tells," may give clues to other players as to the value of an individual's hand.

However, the same "tells" can be manipulated by experienced players to give a false sense of security to opponents, or as a bluff when a tell of confi-dence masks a worthless hand. Thus experienced poker players do not habit-ually judge the tells of other experienced players, only of novices with plenty of money to lose. Yet as a simple precaution, some poker players may wear darkened glasses to hide any tell-tale flickers of their eyes.

The eyes can often "telegraph" our intentions, but can also be used in bluff. For instance, in football, if a striker looks at his supposed target in a particular corner of the net, he will be telegraphing his intentions to the goal-keeper whom is watching the striker for any clue to his next move. However, if the striker knows his eyes are being scrutinised, he will deliberately look in the other direction from where he will send the ball, confusing an overea-ger goalkeeper.

The moral of the story is that the goal-keeper should have judged the situation on the striker's approach and dispatch of the ball, rather than believing the eyes of the crafty player.

The skill of misdirecting the attention of an opponent is widely used in sports, be it in the dribbling skills of football and basketball players, or the overtaking tactics of racing drivers.

However, the real misdirection lies in the true purpose of sports, being to produce vast revenue for shareholders and sporting goods manufacturers, whilst providing the masses with a way to spend their money on taxable pursuits.

Not only are sports such as football/soccer the product of social engineering, it has been said that they are a religion—a true statement considering both football and religion are man-made ways to control the wider populace.

Thus sports can be a political tool to either unite or divide a nation, region or city, and remain a huge source of revenue for many services and industries, such as transport, tourism, clothing manufacturers and alcohol suppliers.

Therefore, the deception of sports is that they exist as sport, when in fact they are the keystone of the textile and beverage industry, a media and advertising compass, the political apron of social manipulation, and a set-square of gambling and betting, all in accordance to the plumb line of money.

If you still think sport is about physical exercise or enjoying a group activity, and matching skills with other players and participants, consider the downfall of England's national football (soccer) team in 2007.

England likes to think of itself as the inventor of football (despite the fact that China invented the game thousands of years ago) and, as former winners of the World Cup in 1966, the English see themselves as a leading light in the international game. However, despite paying their national team's millionaire players ludicrously high salaries, their performance is always rather poor.

In 2007 England was dealt a body blow when it failed to qualify for the Euro 2008 championship playoff, which sees European countries battle it out for the chance to be the continent's best team.

The press reported the misery of both English football fans and the players of the nation alike; however, it was the comments of worried British economists that grabbed my attention. The result of England failing to qualify for Euro 2008 could mean an estimated £2 billion pound loss to the U.K. economy. Why? Because football has little to do with twenty-two men chasing a ball for ninety minutes, and rather more to do with how many tickets are sold to see those men chase that ball for ninety minutes.

Football is about selling expensive clothing with team logos and national flags printed on them. It is about selling airplane flights and train tickets and petrol for family cars. Football is about selling holiday packages and hotel rooms. It is about selling shoes and bags and hats and scarves. It is about selling beer and breakfast cereal and burgers and toys for children of all ages.

Football may even be about uniting the country under the banner of national pride and enjoying a shared culture with the people who live in the same country. It is a political tool and is useful in social engineering. And as I said before, football may even be described as a religion, as players are worshipped as gods, whilst stadiums, arenas and football pitches (or fields) have a similar role to churches.

Football may be all these things, but what it is not, is simply just a sport!

Ask a child playing football with his friends if he is playing the game for fun and to match his skill with friends, or because he dreams about being the next David Beckham or Maradona, rich and famous with cars and houses and girlfriends, and who will be worshipped by millions of fans around the world, and see what answer you get.

To conclude my cynical ideas on deception in sport, let me just remind you of the 2008 Olympic Games in Beijing. If you were one of the millions of viewers around the world who watched the televised opening ceremony of the games, and marvelled at the spectacular fireworks display, don't forget that most of it was a fake. Real fireworks were thought to be too dangerous to be used in inclement weather conditions in the Chinese capital, so most of the display was computer generated and superimposed onto a black sky. It was a colourful deception, designed to add unbelievable wonderment to a huge sporting event. And it was just that, unbelievable! Perhaps one day we will see sports stars and athletes who are also computer generated, thus reducing the chances of them taking bribes to deliberately lose a race, game or match.

Advertising and Sales

As a consumer I am probably in the minority when I say that a product, if it is any good, should sell itself without the need for cheesy advertising campaigns. This is contrary to every rule of advertising, which would suggest that if people don't know a product exists they can't buy it, regardless of how good it is.

However, it is also true that a product that is of a poor standard, or which attracts little demand, certainly needs a great deal more advertising than a quality product which is popular, and perhaps even part of everyday speech. In the U.K. we "Hoover" the floor rather than vacuum it; we use "Scotch Tape," "Sellotape" and a "Stanley-knife" rather than sticky tape and a carpet knife; we drink "Coke" rather than cola; and we cover up mistakes with "Tippex" or "White-Out" rather than with correction fluid, and so on.

Brands such as these have, therefore, become so popular that they have become nouns for specific items, and yet, in the case of Coca-Cola, can still propagate vast amounts of advertising. Obviously Coca-Cola would like to continue it's saturation advertising until all of its rivals have been forgotten.

As one of the planet's most powerful advertisers, Coca-Cola has employed various methods of selling their product over the years, including the use of slogans, jingles, genre iconography, sex-face-celebrity-product association, and apparently the more controversial subliminal advertising, the latter being a deception that Coca-Cola would vehemently deny using, seing that it is illegal.

The slogan "the real thing" highlights just what Coca-Cola believes their product to be, and that any other cola is nothing more than an illegitimate copy. Whilst Coke may well have been the original cola, it certainly does not follow that rival colas are of inferior quality, making the slogan "real thing" slightly erroneous. Pepsi may not be a real Coca-Cola, but it is a real cola.

As Hitler pointed out in *Mein Kampf*, slogans are to be used regularly and simplified as the target population for such slogans increases. Hitler believed that people remember and repeat a slogan more easily than the facts or even the fiction which generated it.

This theory was sadly confirmed by the end of WWII, when most Germans were so shell-shocked that they could only remember that the whole affair had something to do with the Jews, rather than super-inflation and mass unemployment.

As a slogan becomes a popular chant, the need for background information and factual clarity summarised in the slogan decreases. In this way a slogan is a clever deception, as it is reproduced at the expense of the facts, and is thus a useful tool in advertising.

Aside from semantically meaningless slogans such as "whiter than white," advertising slogans often hover just beyond the prosecution of the Trade Descriptions Act. For example, the caffeine rich drink Red Bull claims that it "gives you wings," an obvious metaphor for refreshment and renewed energy levels. However, the drink does not, as it claims, literally result in the growth of wings.

Furthermore, Australians do indeed "give a XXXX" for something else, as Victoria Bitter is one of Australia's leading brands of lager. Moreover, as VB is overshadowed by four-X hyperbole, Carlsberg continues taking liberties with the mathematical concept of probability. The lager is "probably the best, in the world." The "best," in this case, being something that is impossible to ascertain, relying on a value judgement of taste, which will obviously vary from person to person.

"The number one" or "premier company" are slogans that can often mislead consumers. Whilst a company may enjoy the most sales of a certain product, such statistics cannot be taken as a sign of superior quality, which "number one" and "premier" suggest. Indeed, the slogan associated with the supermarket giant Templeton's, explains that quantity is more important than quality in the capitalist society: "Stack 'em high, sell 'em cheap."

Furthermore, in terms of freedom of speech, a company can call themselves whatever they like, without the need for facts to back up their statement.

A man could call himself the world's number one artist, but the qualitative statement would be without meaning. The artist's mother may think he is number one, despite the fact that his art may stink! Therefore, the only way a person or company can truly call themselves "number one" is if they have an address or a name that comes before any other, either numerically or alphabetically. Anything else is just the opinion of those who wish to sell something.

The next step towards reaping the benefits from an annoying, yet curiously effective advertising campaign, is to match a slogan up to an appropriate jingle, or short catchy tune. "Do the Shake and Vac and put the freshness back" is a good example of an annoying jingle that makes people cringe at first, but also directs their hand towards the product on the supermarket shelf.

Thus the catchy or embarrassingly awful jingle not only reminds people of their laughter when they first heard it, but such jingles also serve as a powerful mnemonic, making the name of the product or service hard to forget.

The phenomenon of certain cheesy television adverts being difficult to forget is also increased when a jingle is accompanied by an actor making a fool of himself by dancing in a unique or hysterical fashion. The "I feel like chicken tonight" slogan accompanied with a wing-flapping dance is a good example of this. But who is more foolish, the actor who makes a fool of himself, but gets paid handsomely for doing so, or the fools who buy products because they cannot get the mental picture of the silly dance out of their head?

Therefore, the deception here is that the consumer thinks a company is foolish for advertising its product with a tacky song and dance, but it is he who is the fool. More often than not a consumer will buy the tacky product so he can get a chance to cheer his family up by giving his own rendition of the embarrassing song and dance in his lounge or kitchen. In such cases it is the manufacturers of tacky products who cringe all the way to the bank.

Moving from jingles and slogans, we now come to gimmicks and positive association. Have you ever found yourself watching adverts on TV when your common sense suddenly kicks in and you begin to systematically analyse the short presentations you are witnessing, scene by scene? You may then ask yourself what the relationship between the images and the product is, and what they have in common.

Moreover, some advertising campaigns actually thrive on baffling the public as to the hazy connection between advert and product. This can be seen in the enigmatic "viral marketing," which produces mysterious slogans or symbols in the form of stickers, posters or even graffiti. The idea is that people begin to talk about the weird symbols multiplying in their environment, symbols which are only explained by the advertising agency after several months of mystery and debate.

Although this form of advertising may seem original, it is suggested that the same technique was once used by a Dublin theatre impresario, who claimed he could invent a word which would become an everyday expression. The Dublin man apparently painted the word "Quiz" on doors and walls around the Irish capital, until it was on the lips of every citizen. "What is it?" they all asked. "Exactly that!" replied the impresario. Of course "quiz" is just a contraction of "inquisition."

The desire to be quirky, clever or amusing has often resulted in adverts that are very popular with a target population of consumers, especially if small, furry, cute puppets are present. However, the desire for a product to be viewed as being a winner has also produced toothbrushes racing each other over an assault course, ball-point pens being rammed into tin cans before their use, and small dogs running down the street with a ribbon of toilet paper tied around their neck.

What we have to ask ourselves is whether we want a toothbrush that can run the four minute mile, or clean our teeth properly. Whether we want a pen that can pierce armour, or just work smoothly enough for us to write something, or whether we need a toilet roll that can stretch from the toilet to the next town, when all we require is a length big enough to wipe our rear end.

Association in advertising normally employs the use of popular celebrities, sexually attractive men and women, stunning areas of natural beauty, privileged environments or situations, and the use of people who have honest, friendly faces.

Essentially the thinking behind these associative tools is that people will buy a product if their favourite celebrity, or an honest looking actor, endorses it. The desired effect is that consumers will believe in the reliability of a product that may also provide them with more happiness in life and increased chances of having sex, even if a connection between the product and such desires is unlikely in the extreme.

A sweaty, overweight workman may think he will be more sexually attractive if he buys the shiny new hammer advertised in a tool catalogue by a half-naked girl. In reality, he would stand more chance of having sex with the girl if he hit her over the head with the hammer, and propositioned her whilst she was still stunned. Which is not what a hammer is for.

A hopeful consumer may also be fooled into believing that they will be awarded with sophistication and class if they buy a product associated with royalty, the "jet set," or the extremely rich—an unlikely phenomenon that must greatly amuse the rich and privileged. After all, it is doubtful that a multi-millionaire would really be impressed by a tray full of cheaply crafted chocolates that are mass produced and sold in most corner shops.

The use of a fancy name with an average product, therefore, serves to give consumers the belief that they are enjoying goods associated with millionaires. For instance, the words Royal, Imperial and Regal have been used on everything from soap to cigarettes.

Tobacco companies hold the belief that smokers want to be associated with royalty, playboys, casinos, diplomats and international espionage, rather than cancer, impotence, yellow teeth and clothes that stink of smoke. Embassy, Consulate, Silk Cut, King Edward, Corona and Regal are just some cigarette and cigar titles that allude to the high life. However, aside from the connection of tobacco to money, there may also be a link from a cigarette's name to alcohol, another addictive product.

If we take the cigarette name "Regal," and reverse it, we find "lager." In the middle of the name "Embassy" we discover "bass," in "Drum Tobacco" we find "rum," and we need not look to closely at smoking "Black Russians" to find a link to alcohol. Furthermore, in every "sale" of cigarettes, or otherwise, we will always see the word "ale," either consciously or otherwise.

It is certain, therefore, that the name given to a product has not just been randomly selected, but has been chosen because of its strong connections with people, places or even similar words that inspire confidence or denote success.

In Britain, a product, company or service that is called "Windsor," "Imperial" or "Churchill," could punt its wares at a target population who lived through WWII or who were born shortly afterwards. Old age pensioners would thus trust a life insurance company that has the same name as a trusted British leader or royalty, who helped defend the nation against a Nazi invasion.

"Oh that nice Mr. Montgomery," an old lady might say, "Oh what a lovely man he was. Yes, I think I'll spend £20,000 on a chair made by Montgomery and Company. It's a name to trust."

The deception of reliability given by such companies may be further enhanced by using adverts with a smiling celebrity who tempts potential clients with a glittering trinket, such as a free gold-coloured plastic carriage clock. The promise of gold is a widely used con to entice people into buying a product.

Yet we should also recall Shakespeare's *Merchant of Venice* and the famous clue to something's true identity: "all that glistens is not gold." This is true not only of free carriage clocks handed out by life insurance companies to their senile clients, but also of gold itself, in some cases.

Indeed, men have been deceived for centuries in their quest to find gold by discovering large quantities of iron pyrites in coal seams and river systems around the globe. Unfortunately, brassy yellow iron pyrites are nothing more than "fool's gold."

However, that is not where the deception of gold ends. Popular with the working class masses, 9 carat gold jewellery is the customary body decoration used to make people feel glamorous or rich; after all, if someone can afford to buy a thick, 9 carat gold neck chain, they must be rich. Right? Wrong! Whilst 9 carat gold is certainly not cheap to purchase, 9 carat gold is certainly not gold—a fact both jewellers and the truly rich keep to themselves, hiding their laughter whenever they see lesser mortals proudly showing off their giant sovereign rings and gold-coloured watches.

The problem with gold is that it is very soft and makes the practical use of its pure 24 carat form almost impossible in jewellery. Therefore metal alloy is used to strengthen the gold, making the highest quality gold jewellery at 22 carats.

However, the more alloy, which is used to fashion the increasingly hard jewellery, the less amount of gold is present. Thus, the lowest quality gold is 9 carats, at nine parts gold and fifteen parts metal alloy. Moreover, as 9 carats is only 37.5% gold, it should not really be called gold at all—much like British chocolate, which should actually be known as "vegelate," as it contains more vegetable extracts than cocoa solids.

Maybe gold mixed with metal alloy should be called "Golly" or "Meld," or simply "yellow crap," as one leading 9-carat jewellery manufactured in the UK once suggested.

If you think I'm being unfair and elitist about the purity of gold, and wish to defend your own collection of pretty jewellery, let me ask you a question. If you went to a café and asked for a cherry muffin and the waiter brought you something that was 37.5% muffin and 62.5% house brick, would you complain? Or would you munch on the extremely hard cake until all your teeth were broken?

But please don't misunderstand me, I'm not saying people should only wear real 22 carat gold jewellery. I'm saying if someone buys gold, it should be gold! Otherwise don't bother buying "gold," but buy gold-coloured metal at a fraction of the cost. Gold-coloured metal is just as aesthetically pleasing as the real article. Rhinestones sparkle like diamonds and coloured glass baubles are as pretty as rubies and sapphires.

So why spend a fortune on a ruby when a piece of red crystal will look just as nice? Why spend thousands on a solid gold Rolex when a gold-coloured watch looks identical, and costs far less? You don't need "real" jewellery if something affordable looks just as nice.

Remember gold is just a metal. It has lasting properties and is useful to science in many ways, but it is just a metal. Its colour can be mimicked, so its value lies in its rarity. But this itself is a deception. If they ever found the lost golden city of El Dorado or the Apache gold in "Canyon del Oro," do you think they'd tell us about the discovery? After all, if we each had a shed full of gold, its value and price would diminish. In case of the collapse of a country's economy and currency, governments have to keep something valuable with which to use in place of money. Gold is usually this safety net. Hence the reason why the gold in Fort Knox never leaves the building and why it is protected by armed troops at all times. Telling the world about the discovery of a gold mountain is not in the best interest of any government, and will not be something you will hear on the news as long as the planet is ruled by money.

Aside from associating a product with a valuable commodity such as gold, or a trustworthy person such as Winston Churchill, product or company names can also contain puns and phonemes. "Ocean Finance," for example, is not only associated with a powerful sea and, therefore, equated with a powerful business, its name also contains the sound of the word "fine," in "finance."

"Admiral Insurance" is associated with someone who is in charge and who commands respect, but also sounds like the word "admire," whilst "Charmin" toilet tissue looks and sounds strikingly similar to the word "charming." "Forest Furnishings" not only rolls off the tongue in an alliterative metre, it also conjures up images of pine tables and chairs in the middle of a wooded clearing, as strong as the surrounding trees, with floral cushions and coverings as soft as the leafy forest floor.

But the true message that the company wishes to emphasise is partially obscured in the name. "Forest Furnishings," could also be "for rest furnishings." In this case the word "rest" is attractive to the eye of the person who wants to buy a comfortable seat to recline on.

In general, however, there are words that we all find attractive and will make us happier. And if we're happier we'll spend our money on things that will sustain the feeling. Attractive words are: NEW, EASY, FREE, HEALTH, MONEY and SEX. See for yourself just how many television adverts for life insurance policies use actors who say some or all of these words in their smiling speeches.

Another key aspect of advertising, especially concerning the marketing of supermarket products and fast food, is the artwork on the cover of boxes, packaging and illustrated menus. The deception here is particularly cruel insofar as it is the society's poorest members' staple diet of the cheap ready-made meals and snack food that is advertised as a gourmet banquet.

Packaging boasts pictures of the exotic meal in question as being lovingly prepared, with an abundance of mouth-watering ingredients. The reality, of course, is that anything that is mass produced will be thrown together without care, and possibly without a substantial potion of meat or vegetables. Moreover, the legend "Serves 2" on the box often transpires to be completely false, unless the two unnamed people are a dieting duo suffering from anorexia.

To continue the deception, many of the packaging photographs of ready meals have been doctored. In the photography, studio pies and other pastries can be stuffed with cotton wool to pad them out a bit more, whilst other food can be coloured, varnished and painted for the required effect of making them more desirable. Computer art software and colour enhancement of the final photo then eradicates any remaining doubt that the product will be unsatisfactory.

The problem of buying something because its image looked attractive on the packaging, but not in reality, is annoying, but not all together surprising. Very rarely have I purchased an item that was a dopple-ganger of its picture. However, even more disturbing than buying something that does not look like its marketed image, is buying it because of something unseen, at least not consciously.

Thus the phenomenon of subliminal advertising poses a threat to those who like to think they are buying something from an expression of free will, and not because they were forced to do so by a trigger that bypassed their conscious sense of cognition.

Although officially frowned upon by advertising companies, and illegal in most Western countries, subliminal advertising may be used more often than is commonly assumed. Whilst tachistoscopic images have been banned—these being pictures or messages flashed up on a cinema or television screen for a moment, to be seen only by the subconscious mind—other subliminal images in full and constant view remain in sight.

Indeed, there are three elements that are most commonly used to provide subliminal advertising suggestions. These are the use of faces, phalluses and the letters "S," "E" and "X" in succession. The letters "F" "U" "C" "K" have also been successful, and are in current use by clothing retailers; for example, "French Connection UK"(FCUK).

Being that humans are highly influenced by non-verbal communication, especially by the expressions of the face, it is not uncommon to see adverts where a product is placed directly beside a smiling face. The face, therefore, gives approval to the consumer's use of the product.

However, in subliminal advertising the pearly white smile of an actor's face is replaced by artwork that suggests a face bearing the same emotion of happiness, but which is cleverly hidden or disguised. For example, depending on how one views such, in the fancy lettering of Coca Cola we can see cartoon faces of two men taking turns to snort a line of cocaine up their nose, perhaps making an association with the drink's historical ingredients, or even its addictive quality.

In other products, faces can be found hidden amongst ice cubes, in the case of whisky and spirits, or placed in such a way as to look at a product with approving eyes.

On a recent holiday in Spain I found a bottle of mineral water that had a supposedly innocent drawing of snow-covered mountains behind the product's name. However, on closer inspection I found that one of the mountains was actually a smiling face that had its mouth open, presumably in anticipation of a cool drink of water.

My journey across Spain also uncovered a tin of paella that had the remaining two elements of subliminal artwork on its packaging. Not only did the photograph on the box show a plate of chicken paella, a fork and a glass of wine, it also showed the word "sex" and the glands of a human penis. The word sex had been fashioned from rice and peppers, whilst the gland was present as a ghostly reflection on the back of the stainless steel fork.

I also saw an advert for Budweiser lager showing the beverage being poured from a bottle. Yet it could be argued that the stream of lager made a smiling face, and the name of the lager actually read "Budwei-sex," which is subtle but effective advertising. It certainly made me want to drink a few bottles of the stuff.

Don't take my word for it though, buy a bottle of Budweiser, look at the writing on the label, and ask yourself if it says "Budweiser" or "Budwei-sex." Also look at the strangely fashioned letter "B"; does it resemble a cartoon penis entering in a cartoon vagina? You tell me.

Perhaps you are quite sceptical about this latter revelation concerning subliminal advertising. Perhaps you suppose that such sexual images are only the creation of an individual's corrupt imagination, and not the artistic policy of major companies. Perhaps you are correct, but it is wise to be forewarned of such a possibility existing.

Could it just be a coincidence that companies such as "Sussex Express Xerox" could seem more attractive than rival photocopying firms, simply because the word sex is repeated throughout the name? It is bad enough when the word "sex" or phallic shapes are discovered on boxes of food or in company names, but it is rather sinister when one discovers such images and words on products marketed to children.

The cigarette brand "Camel" has, for instance, been accused of such marketing, albeit unofficially and without any legal prosecution. The fluorescent colours found on the cartoon posters heralding the latest "cool" exploit of

Camel's camel, is perhaps empowered to a greater degree by its facial characteristics resembling both male and female genitalia.

Perhaps the tobacco company goes even further by hiding a naked man, who holds his erect penis, on the front of their cigarette cartons. The man is discovered if one looks at the dromedary's front leg for a long enough time. Coincidence? Perhaps, but is it also a coincidence that the name Camel may seem rather attractive to younger smokers, as it bears a striking resemblance to the word "caramel." Perhaps in this way it is children who are the most susceptible to subliminal advertising, because the natural barriers of suspicion have yet to be formed by adult experience.

If you look at the whole advertising industry in general, I think you will find it difficult to detect any traces of morality. If a product is being bought by children, illegally or not, then it will be marketed to children, regardless of the harmful effects that the product may have on young minds and bodies. Profit is the initial concern of ad company clients, not the foundations of a healthy society.

The total neglect of morality, decency and honesty is not the exclusive vice of advertising agencies, however. Almost every salesman in the world has, at one time or another, chosen to add a pinch of sheer dishonesty to his personal endorsement of the product or service he is desperately trying to sell.

Thus deceptions used by salesmen and women to fool their money-laden quarry vary from using the aroma of freshly ground coffee to sell a house, to more complicated scams and frauds that are highly illegal. However, in between the innocent and the illegal are a myriad of sales techniques that require either a straight face or a strong personality to employ effectively.

Due to the psychological phenomenon of "assumed similarity bias," a salesman who looks and sounds like the customer whom he is chatting to, is automatically trusted to a certain extent. Trust can be further increased by the salesman's ability to mimic body language and give the signs of someone who is friendly and honest, this being because most of us are fooled by appearances.

The next trick in the salesman's arsenal is to get a "foot in the door." In Islamic countries a "foot in the door" could be the invitation by a bazaar merchant to join him for a cup of refreshing apple tea. The idea is that the merchant gives a customer a small glass of hot sugary tea, and the thankful customer repays the kind gesture by giving the merchant lots of money for an expensive rug. This informal tea break relaxed the customer, made him feel welcome and respected, but also made him feel obliged to pay back his host's kindness by spending money in his shop.

In other situations, the foot in the door technique can see customers accepting a trial or free sample of a small or inexpensive product. If they like the product they will be more likely to buy something, which usually turns out to be larger and more expensive than the free sample. In other words, if a customer has one good experience with a company or salesman, they will probably agree to further product trials and an eventual purchase.

Unlike the foot in the door, the "Door in the Face" technique occurs when a salesman deliberately sets the price of a service or product at a ludicrously high level. Thus the customer immediately puts an end to any speculation of a purchase being made. It is at this point that the salesman drastically reduces the price, and perhaps throws added extras in free of charge.

The customer then believes they have the upper hand and happily agrees to the sale. The deception, of course, was that the true price was always lower than that originally stated. Indeed, this deception is quite similar to the whole concept of sales and reductions to clear. For example, if you want £100 for something, you put a label on it stating that its price is usually £200, but is being sold for 50% less, for a short time only. People always like a bargain!

But remember that even if you do get a bargain, there may be hidden costs that were not advertised or even mentioned by grinning sales staff. Low cost airlines are especially guilty of hitting customers with hidden costs, not least of which are the wide range of taxes and insurance charges associated with air travel. Some budget airlines continue to infuriate passengers who arrive at airport check-in desks with their luggage, only to discover they are to be charged a fortune because their bags are too heavy. I mean, if you're going on holiday and pack more than a toothbrush, a towel and one change of underwear in your bag, then expect to be penalised for bringing too much. So, a low cost airline ticket simply means that there will be a high baggage charge, or that food and beverages served on board the aircraft will be sold at extortionate prices, $25 for a tuna sandwich and £15 for a Coke.

Another technique that is used to trick customers into making a purchase is that of insulting their financial standing. For example, a customer is told by a sneering salesman that they can't afford to buy the object that they have been admiring. The customer is insulted and feels the need to prove the salesman wrong by purchasing the item. Then the salesman perhaps blushes and feigns embarrassment, until the customer leaves his shop.

Even though the customer thinks they got the better of a condescending shop assistant, they have actually fallen for one of the oldest sales tricks; tell someone they can't have something and they'll want it even more. Anyone who has children will be fully aware of this phenomenon, and yet they themselves will fall victim to their desire to possess that which is forbidden or deemed to be out of their price range.

Aside from the aforementioned techniques that are universally unsheathed by sales staff, someone can also achieve a successful sale with an overbearing nature or strong personality. Many people have in the past signed contracts with bullying salesmen, just to get such people out of their home. Furthermore, people will agree to a purchase or contract over the phone, rather than deal with a salesman face to face.

In conclusion, a salesman will dress in a manner that makes him look successful, and therefore reliable. He may drive an expensive car and have the nicest smile you've ever seen. A salesman may also act like one of your best friends or the son you never had. He may attempt to mirror your body language and establish good rapport by talking about something of personal interest to a customer. For instance, if he finds out his customer is a dentist, he will talk about teeth.

Everyone likes to feel in control of a situation, and discussing one's profession with a stranger promotes a sense of personal happiness and achievement. And if you're happy you'll spend money more easily. But don't be fooled, the only reason the salesman is talking to you in the first place is because he believes his friendliness will be rewarded with a sale, and ultimately a juicy commission.

If you keep the true nature of your relationship with a salesman in mind, you will be more inclined to better consider everything that you are told, before either making a purchase or parting company with your wallet remaining unmolested.

Do not look down on salesmen, however, for selling is an art, which the mercantile tradition derives from time immemorial. Indeed, you can perhaps admire the talent of someone who has persuaded you to buy some piece of crap, especially if you knew it was a piece of crap even before you bought it. If you find yourself in such a situation you may even ask yourself if you have just fallen for a subtle yet effective form of mind control.

Moreover, studies have shown that people who are honest generally move their arms and hands in expressive gestures, to physically emphasis what they are saying. Yet people who are lying to us make no such gestures. Therefore, those who have mastered the art of body language, and how to manipulate it for nefarious purposes, can fool us by mimicking honest non-verbal communication.

Apart from using sophisticated techniques of psychological manipulation, a good salesman will point out the flaws of an object before the customer gets the chance. But the twist is that they will make the flaws seem like advantages.

"Don't worry madam, the gaping hole in the side of the car door is designed to let oxygen in so you don't die of carbon monoxide poisoning, and it can be used as an escape hatch if you have an accident."

"But I have no money to buy the car."

"Don't worry madam, I'll arrange credit."

A bad salesman, on the other hand, may well convince a customer to buy something, and remove all doubt they had about its purchase, but will then let the customer walk out of his shop and buy the same item next door.

Good or bad, salesmen are neither angels or demons, they are simply trying to make a living. They can't force you to buy anything that you don't want to buy. But when the shopping channel is on TV, and the phone is right beside us, and we've got a new credit card, and they will deliver to your door, and we could do with a new table to replace that old one in the living room... then we may recall too late that a fool and his money are easily parted.

Art

As previously mentioned, theatre artists and set designers have used Trompe l'Oeil back cloths to deceive the eye, making the audience believe they are seeing a larger perspective than actually exists on stage; for example, the appearance of a landscape stretching far into the distance. However, the modern use of this skill is also employed by interior design consultants, who make small rooms in their client's home look more spacious than they really are.

Architects, too, enjoy this skill, using deception to make buildings more attractive to the eye. They do this by designing highly decorative facades, or mirrored windows that reflect surrounding buildings; especially useful in a city that has classical architecture that may be spoilt by the presence of a looming tower, with its huge block of grey concrete.

Moreover, the very geometric structure of a building can be manipulated to appear more pleasing to the eye. The Parthenon of 5th Century Greece is one of the world's most aesthetically pleasing Doric temples, but it is in fact not quite as symmetric as it would seem. Its great pillars slope inwards whilst its marble stairs are curved.

However, the eye is tricked into seeing straight lines on a beautiful building without flaw, or at least it would have been without flaw if it had not been blown up by the Venetian army in 1687. Sadly, the building is but a shadow of its former glory, with its marble scattered across the Acropolis and its priceless friezes lying far away in the British Museum.

In the traditional art of painting and drawing, deception has been used to create the illusion of light, sloping perspective and three-dimensional images. It has even been possible for artists to devise paintings that appear to be nothing more than smears of colour, but which are actually inverted portraits when viewed with a reflective cylinder. The ingenuity of artists has made it possible to produce the seemingly impossible. *The Devil's Tuning Fork* is such an "impossible" creation, which appears to have three prongs, until a closer inspection highlights only two.

The Dutch graphic artist, Maurits Escher, specialised in such impossibilities in his work, and was able to draw fantastic scenes of buildings that appeared to defy the laws of physics. Artificial waterfalls dropping down from a height onto the same level from which they sprang, for example. Or, ladders that allowed people to climb up to the level on which the bottom of the same ladder was rooted.

Another master of deception in art was the great surrealist painter, Salvador Dalí, a man whose eccentric life of perversion and genius became an artwork in itself. Fascinated with many aspects of psychology, Dalí became familiar with the Gestalt laws of organisation, a psychological principle designed to understand the concept of illusion.

Essentially, these laws or principles follow the maxim that "the whole is greater than the sum of its parts." We see familiar objects and geometric shapes as a whole, completed, and in groups and patterns, rather than incomplete, missing outlines or in random placement and juxtaposition.

Dalí manipulated the Gestalt principle of closure to create amazing optical illusions and double images. In his paintings, titled *Spain* and *The Invisible Man*, two figures are recognised purely because of the human ability to join broken lines with our mind. These mentally completed lines therefore let us see human subjects, where no such figures exist.

By using shadow and various objects similar to each other in shape, Dalí was also able to create double images, where if we look at the work long enough we will see something completely different. For instance, in *The Image Disappears* we see a woman who is reading a book, but who soon changes into a large portrait of Vermeer's face.

Another good example of this double image technique is also found in the self-explanatory *Slave Market with the Disappearing Bust of Voltaire*. So great was his interest in double images and deceiving the eye that Dalí even tried to create a military camouflage that relied on his own special theories on optical illusions.

A little known deception in the world of classical art, which I'm sure Dalí would have found amusing, is the possibility that the many gold statues and busts found in museums may not in fact be made of gold at all, not even 9-carat faux gold from high-street jewellers. Yet the notion of gold statues actually being made of electroplated silver seems beyond comprehension, at least to museum curators who have spent a fortune collecting gold statues.

However, in 1936 such a theory was aroused with the discovery of what became known as the Baghdad Battery, a small clay pot of Middle-Eastern origin, dated 1,800 years before electricity was harnessed in the western world. The Baghdad device consists of a pot, an oxidised iron rod and a copper sheath. When an alkaline, or acidic solution such as grape juice is poured into the jug, a small electric charge is produced. Although the charge is too small to power motors or generators, it has been proved to be suitable for the process of electroplating.

In experiments with the Baghdad Battery, a small silver statue was immersed in a solution of gold-cyanide. The grape juice battery was then able to cover the statue in a thin veneer of gold. Therefore, if the battery was indeed used for such purposes, it brings the possibility of western alchemists actually electroplating silver with gold-cyanide, rather than finding occult ways to change lead to gold. Moreover, if the Baghdad device is indeed a battery, and not just assumed to be such by imaginative archaeologists, poor old Galvani and Volta lose their historical credit for being battery pioneers.

It is not just classical and ancient art that may hold many mysteries as yet uncovered or unexplained, modern art also reeks of deception. For those of us who admire art in its traditional guise, for example, a masterpiece painted on canvas, or an expertly crafted marble statue, we may conclude that the modern deception commonly used in art circles is of conceptual art. When an "artist" claims that their bed, tent, rubbish bin, pile of bricks or empty room is art, serious consideration must be given to the use of the word "Art."

What is art? Is it something pleasing to the eye, or is it something that provokes shock and heated debate? Is the best art the colourful crayon scribbling of our young children, because it is honest and an innocent representation of the world? Is a pile of crap conceptual art, or is conceptual art just a pile of crap?

The problem with art is that nobody really knows what it is. However, "Art," with a capital "A," is probably a bowl of custard placed on a marble pedestal in an empty white room, whilst "art" is that nice painting in your grandmother's house of somewhere sunny, which reminds you of your holidays, and makes you happy on a rainy day. But even here there is a problem. Art is not what I think it is, but what you think it is. Silly millionaires buy blank canvases because they are told it is art by sniggering gallery owners. Therefore, whilst the skill and techniques used in art can be taught, the philosophical concept of art cannot.

Art? If you have to ask you will never know.

Crime

As old as civilisation itself, crime has proven to be an enduring cornucopia of lies and deception. From the time the first dishonest caveman passed off dog meat as a prime cut of antelope, men have been dreaming up ways to pull the wool over their neighbours' eyes. Aside from rape, murder and theft, the earliest crime inflicted upon society was possibly trade related, bartering supposedly quality goods for items made from cheap and unreliable materials.

Modern technology has given police the ability to log fingerprints, detect the smallest trace of blood, and hunt criminals with heat detectors and night-sights. Forensic scientists have been blessed with the knowledge of DNA, in which a single hair can give the identity of either a victim or a murderer. However, as suggested by Sherlock Holmes, it is still the crimes that rely on the least amount of ingenuity and cunning which are the hardest to detect. Elaborate crimes shed more suspicious clues than crimes that are commonplace and simple.

For example, a suspected murderer took his wife for a walk by the seaside. It seems that he found a nice high cliff and suddenly pushed her over the edge. Then he went to the nearest phone box and called the police and an ambulance.

"She was just having a look over the edge when she slipped," he said.

It was never suggested that he had a motive for murder, such as their neighbours hearing them shouting at each other only days before the "accident," so the police had little reason to suspect him (despite the suspicions of his wife's family).

Yet, if he had driven his wife to the same cliff top, cracked her skull open with a hammer, poured petrol over her body, set fire to the car and pushed it over the edge, he would have gone too far. The police would have immediately asked why she decided to drive to a cliff top in the first place, why her charred remains showed signs of violence, and why she was fried in petrol, when the car she was driving used diesel. In other words, the best crimes are the most simplistic, and possibly the ones that have yet to be solved or even discovered.

Some of the most effective crimes rely on the widely held belief that if we are conned, at least we didn't get stung for too much money. For instance, if we put a dollar or pound coin in a charity box, we won't be too upset if we are then told that there is no such charity. We may feel sorry for legitimate charities who might suffer because of such despicable cons, but we won't be too heartbroken.

However, that is exactly what criminals want us to think. If they tried to make us give them $30 dollars to their bogus charity our suspicions would certainly have been aroused, but what harm is there in giving away $1? The harm is not only that it's a dollar less for real charities, it's a dollar added to a dollar added to two or three hundred other dollars. Cents add up to dollars and dollars add up to a master criminal's villa in Miami or Spain.

Charity swindles are made even more unfortunate when some of the genuine charities themselves channel money away from those who need it the most. A few years ago a famous children's charity paid off a large shopping debt belonging to a member of the British royal family, who was the charity's patron. This action put me off from giving money to any charity since.

Contrary to popular belief, crime is not frowned upon by the majority of society, and is perhaps even encouraged. After all, what the law deems to be a crime, and what the people of the land view as being criminal are two very different things in many cases. A child murderer is a criminal; only a handful of mentally ill deviants would disagree. But is someone who smokes cannabis a criminal?

As the widespread smoking of marijuana is found in every class and social strata, it would be lunacy to arrest and brand everyone who has ever smoked a joint as being a criminal. Furthermore, the stability of prison security would be on shaky grounds if inmates did not have access to cannabis, or any other drug required to appease the violent, aggressive and addicted.

If this is true then it raises the question of there being crimes that are ignored by the police and governmental agencies. The answer is of course there are crimes that are ignored by the police; domestic violence, under age drinking and prostitution being but three such crimes. It would simply not be possible to imprison every violent husband, drunken teenager and call girl in the country, either from the practicalities of prison space or because of the time it would take to prosecute such "criminals" in court.

Therefore, criminal prosecutions are directly related to public tolerance. If the public doesn't care, the police won't either, but if there is a public outcry, both police and politicians will suddenly find themselves in hot water until they take action.

One cause of public outcry and extensive media attention is the smuggling and illegal transportation of immigrants and political asylum seekers. Attracted by the employment opportunities in the United States or the welfare benefit system in the United Kingdom, illegal immigrants and asylum seekers, who succeed in slipping under the noses of customs and passport officials, have often done so at great risk and expense. Many illegal immigrants have endured long hours in cramped, dangerous and inhospitable conditions, be it hiding in the back of an articulated lorry, a ship's cargo container, or even clinging to the landing gear of an aircraft.

Bizarrely, two young men once tried to enter the UK by climbing inside a jumbo jet's gear bay, before a seven-hour flight from Pakistan. One of the men froze to death, whilst the other spent time in hospital, before being deported. In the case of being taken into a country whilst hiding in the back of a truck, knowledge of old border crossing tricks from previous wars may be a valuable aid to would-be smugglers.

For instance, all policemen and border guards are human, and thus have human failings. No-one wants to inspect a van or truck that is literally covered in shit. Be it manure, road tar, paint or other unpleasant substances, no guard really wants to get his nice clean uniform all messed up. Yes, there are sniffer dogs to do the dirty work, but dogs only go where their handlers go. And if a dog handler can't be bothered climbing over a cargo of slimy oil drums to hunt for illegal immigrants, the smugglers have won yet another round of their dangerous game.

Amongst its great arsenal of deception, the art of smuggling utilises methods that are both simple and sophisticated to transport illegal contraband— hiding things in hollowed-out objects or swallowing plastic capsules filled with drugs, being the more complicated and risky strategies.

Like the best of crimes, the simple smuggling methods are also the best. Why risk a "Colombian Pellet" full of cocaine or heroine bursting in your stomach, and suffering a painful death as a result, when you could legally import a whole ship full of drugs, be they disguised or not?

Aside from the fact that drugs can be liquefied and imported inside cans of soup or bottles of whisky, and that real guns can be smuggled alongside legal replicas, the right customs officials can easily be bribed to doctor the import/export documents in your favour. The bigger the operation, the higher the bribe. No matter how trustworthy a customs officer may be, everyone has their price.

For the individual smuggler with a limited budget, the smuggling of ancient artefacts offers plenty of opportunities for adventure, travel and a modest profit. For example, if a crafty art dealer were to travel to Athens and purchase an ancient bust or statue from a black market source, a simple deception could follow. He would simply paint the object with the cheapest paint and gold leaf that he could find.

Then he would be required to convince Greek customs officials that he purchased the grotesque object at an inexpensive market stall, a place where similar objects are sold by the thousands to swarms of rich tourists in search of any crappy old souvenir on their holiday. Normal customs officials would laugh at the smuggler and his worthless tat, wondering why he had bothered buying such rubbish.

Back home safely, all the smuggling art dealer would have to do is clean the ancient artefact of its paint, and sell it to the highest bidder.

Aside from buying goods that have obviously been smuggled into a county, the public also perpetuates the supply and demand for counterfeit goods. Whilst attempts to forge national currency are constantly being thwarted by complicated changes to its design, the simple copying of designer goods remains unhindered. Such goods are the source of much deception.

We may feel that buying a counterfeit "designer" shirt and a "Rolex" for a fraction of the conventional price is a harmless bargain. However, there are several points to consider here. Politicians may tell the public that jobs are being lost in the clothing manufacturing industry, for example, due to the sale of counterfeit goods. But what they may fail to say is that both counterfeit and genuine designer clothes are probably being manufactured in China, India or Taiwan, where workers get paid a pittance—an attractive situation for companies in America or Britain that desire to raise profits by lowering the salary of their workers. These are the same government-backed companies who close down factories and production plants in the expensive West, and reopen them in the cheap East, with a smiling face and a box of fresh exploitation.

If a factory in China employs virtual slaves to make products bound for the West, this situation is bad enough. Yet it gets worse if the factory is churning out fake and counterfeit goods. Such wares are inexpensive and affordable, yet may also be dangerous. Thus the real problem with counterfeit goods comes when they are products intended for children that are poorly manufactured, and are made without regard to fire retardation or a child's safety.

Moreover, goods intended for human consumption can be lethal. Fake vodka produced in Eastern Europe has been found to contain both urine and anti-freeze, a vile cocktail that can cause death to those who drink it.

Being that humans are a lazy species of animal, we like to receive gains and profits with the least amount of work, investment or effort being expended. It is because of this desire that we are willing to participate in all manner of get-rich-quick schemes and gambling. However, such schemes and ventures are, unfortunately, often the product of companies who also want maximum profits for the least amount of effort on their behalf. Thus deception is again called into play.

Get-rich-quick scams can include home worker kits and pyramid schemes, the latter being a mathematical con where people are invited to make an investment in an individual's scheme, and in turn expect to receive money from twenty other investors. However, as more and more investors come into the pyramid it becomes impossible to find enough people who are willing to participate, and thus losses by those near the bottom of the pyramid are incurred. Home-worker scams, on the other hand, whilst not requiring a high monetary investment, are cruel insofar as they demand hard work with no thanks or reward, and almost certain losses.

Such scams could, for example, include the assembly of car alarm kits, wicker craft work or painting by numbers portraits. The kits are purchased by individuals from home-worker companies for a "modest" fee and are sent back to the company when completed.

The theory is that the more kits one buys and completes, the more kits one can sell, and the more profit one will make. Unfortunately, after being bought and returned, none of the completed kits are ever accepted and sold by home-worker companies. No matter how professionally completed, such work will always be deemed to be "poor quality" and "unfit for sale."

In the case of free gift or holiday scams, the deception is obvious since nothing is free in this world. Perhaps the con could be as simple as informing someone that they can benefit from free accommodations in Greece, for a small processing or booking fee. Of course, by the time the poor holiday maker arrives at their Grecian destination, they will discover that their villa is abandoned and the holiday company has supposedly gone bankrupt.

The free gift or holiday scam can be as simple as posting a prize-claim phone number to a "lucky" winner. Such winners usually coming from poorer areas where anything free would be welcome, and thus more tempting. When the unfortunate person phones the prize hotline number they will discover that they must pay a premium rate to listen to an answering machine giving them longwinded details of their free pen or blank cassette tape. In some cases no free pens are encountered, but the caller is instead confronted with an hour long recording of a friendly, engaging message. The deception here is that the person phoning for their prize thinks they have yet to get through to the hotline, and are waiting for the phone to be answered, but are actually running up a huge bill.

Gambling gives us our final category of pursuits that are seen to give big profits from small investments. Contrary to popular belief, casinos do not cheat or swindle customers with trick roulette wheels or Black Jack dealers using sleight of hand. The law of averages and mathematical probability ensures the casino will always make a profit.

Gambling on sporting events is not quite so certain, with regard to probability. In football, goalkeepers can let balls deliberately slip through their fingers and into the net, in horse racing a jockey can pull up his steed, in cricket entire teams can give shoddy performances, whilst in boxing dishonest pugilists can take a fall.

It is a peculiar thing about human nature that geniuses can create works of art, invent devices to make our lives easier and make brilliant scientific discoveries, and yet can also use their intellectual gift to commit crimes. Thus the latest computer technology, whilst being ingenious, entertaining, labour saving and helpful, can also be abused by devious computer boffins. Not only can undeniably clever hackers cause irritation and annoyance to everyone with a PC or laptop, they can also undermine national security by breaking into computers linked to military defence networks.

Moreover, computer viruses named after one of the oldest military deceptions in literature, the "trojan horse," can cause havoc to computers owned by both multinational companies and little old ladies alike. Such viruses pretend to be emails and slip into hard disc drives when opened by a user. Inside the computer they begin to steal passwords, dismantle shortcuts to programmes and generally make life more miserable for the user, not to mention the fact that the virus in question escapes and spreads to everyone to whom you've ever sent an email.

Although anti-virus software is available to combat such trojan horses, worms and other computer infections, the horrifying deception could be that the same companies who produce anti-virus software are the same companies who spread viruses in the first place. The idea is to invent a disease and then sell the cure—perhaps the perfect crime.

Another seemingly perfect crime stems from buying second computers that have had their previous user's information deleted, or at least that's what the previous owner believes. Data recovery software can restore "deleted" information by looking deep within the computer's hard drive for hidden files, if they have not been subject to many "passes" of anti-recovery software. Even "overwritten" data can still be recovered by using Magnetic Force Microscopy (MFM) and Scanning Probe Microscopy (SPM) techniques.

So when you get rid of an old computer, remove its hard drive and smash it to smithereens. Otherwise some joker with data recovery software may end up perusing through all the private and confidential information that you had stored on your computer. With this information the dishonest funster can enact identity fraud or sell your private details to his criminal contacts. Where you live, how much money you have in the bank, your bank details and passwords, etc., can all be accessed; gigabytes of information you'd rather not share.

What fun those jolly computer hackers must have, though. Especially the ones who use your expensive broadband internet access, by logging onto you account for free. How? By sitting outside or next door to your house and abusing the invisible hospitality of your computer's wireless connection. Unless your connection is encrypted and users have to have a password to access it, any cheeky hacker can log on, and reduce your broadband speed and capability. Aside from freely accessing the internet, a skilled hacker can also access your desktop facility and wade through your private folders and documents for his own amusement.

Internet crime has given rise to both the sick pedalling of child pornography and "grooming," plus a wealth of scams and cons. The vile nature of the former crime is so obvious it does not warrant further discussion, however, the latter crimes should perhaps be explained to save you the embarrassment of being caught out.

Essentially, if it is too good to be true, it is not true. You have not won a million pounds or free airline tickets or free holidays, so do not phone any prize-line telephone numbers. But most of all, do not give your credit card or PIN (Personal Identification Number) details to anyone on the internet. It is just a recipe for disaster. I would also hesitate to make my own web page, blog or give details to such networking sites as "Facebook" or "Myspace." Identity theft is a growing problem and the more personal information that we post on the Net, the easier it becomes.

Do not pay to enter a prize drawing, and do not answer any "Nigerian Letters" asking you for permission to transfer money into your bank account.

The internet is not a safe playground, and no one inside can be trusted.

Any good university student or researcher knows that the Internet is not a reliable source, as all cyberspace IDs can be easily faked. It doesn't take a genius to cut and paste from an official Web site, using HTML knowledge, to start a bogus page.

Indeed, IDs in general cannot be fully trusted. If someone comes to your door and shows you a card that says he works for the electricity board or electric company, and that he requires to come inside to read the meter, what guarantee is there that he is not a burglar or rapist? None! Absolutely none! If you phone the number on his ID card, and someone from the electricity board replies, it may well just be his accomplice. Only two people are needed to make the phone number "real."

The situation is further aggravated if the caller is wearing a uniform that you believe he could not possess if he were not the person he said he was. For instance, if a man in a police uniform comes to your door, do you really want to phone the local police station, or do you let him in and offer him a cup of tea? Police, army, or security guard uniforms can be easily purchased in mail order catalogues, as can fake IDs!

Remember, bogus callers are especially fond of those who are trusting and unquestioning, elderly, partially sighted, infirm, weak or disabled, or even those you are simply impressed by ID cards or uniforms. But even the most sceptical of us can be caught out if we have no reason to suspect the credentials of a caller are phoney.

However, the sad fact is that, in order for society to function, there has to be a time when we do indeed trust that someone is who they say they are, without having a Spanish Inquisition. Spending half an hour phoning up the electricity board's HQ to confirm an ID, every time a man comes to read the meter, simply isn't going to work. Criminals understand this better than anyone.

Bogus callers who are actually burglars or, in the worst case scenario, rapists are bad enough, but consider a stranger who appears at the door and claims to be a long lost relative. Without proof to the contrary, the impostor may well intend to parasite off someone until they die, leaving all they have to the impostor in a newly amended will.

Throughout history there have been many famous cases of people claiming to be someone else in order to gain inheritance, a title, or even a job. In recent years there was a German psychiatric patient who claimed to be Grand Duchess Anastasia, the murdered daughter of Russia's Tsar Nicholas II. If her claims had proven to be true, this madwoman would have inherited her right to the Russian throne, should it ever return.

Despite surviving members of the Romanov family actually confirming her identity, Anna Anderson was proven to be a fake when a sample of her DNA was shown not to match that of any European Royalty, an impossibility for a true Romanov.

Another case of an impostor pretending to be someone whom they are not in order to achieve money or success was that of Brian MacKinnon. MacKinnon, also known as "Brandon Lee," was an academically inept medical student who had been forced to leave Glasgow University due to poor exam results. Refusing to believe he could no longer fulfil his dream of being a doctor, MacKinnon, a man in his thirties, decided to return to high school in order to get better qualifications, and reapply to medical school.

The unusual factor about this bizarre case was not so much that the teenagers in MacKinnon's class did not tell instantly that he was a grown man, but rather that the school teachers did not suspect his true identity. He had, after all, attended the same school legitimately fifteen years previously, and many members of the staff were still working there.

Although he looked like an adult, MacKinnon explained his appearance as being the result of a skin condition that caused premature aging, and his adult outlook on life as being the result of a private education in Canada. Brandon Lee's self belief in his new identity was thus so strong that he convinced others that he was a genuine schoolboy. MacKinnon's story certainly proves that appearances can be deceiving, and should be a warning to us all that we cannot trust anything, based on appearance alone.

A final example of this problem can be shown by a case in England in which criminals were fed up with stealing bank cards from those who stood at ATM machines, withdrawing cash. They were bored watching PIN numbers being typed in before trying to distract the unsuspecting person's attention by saying they had dropped money on the ground, then running off with their card. It was simply too much hard work.

So, with typical villainous ingenuity and cheek, the criminals decided to hire an empty shop premise, which they redecorated to resemble a small bank, with a fully working ATM machine. The difference was that this ATM recorded the PIN numbers of those who used it, but neither returned the cards nor dispensed any money—simple, but effective.

Chapter Three

DECEPTION IN COMBAT AND WAR

Combat and war tactics have changed vastly since Bronze Age armies of classical Greece inspired the tales outlined in *The Iliad*; however, one thing remains constant. The use of deception is both paramount to a warrior's victory over his opponent, and necessary for political manoeuvres, whether it be the use of visual camouflage, or verbally dragging a nation into war to find "weapons of mass destruction" where none exist.

Being that necessity is the mother of invention, and that food and the defence of one's life are two of the prime necessities, deception in combat and warfare became vital to the earliest civilisations. Man the hunter not only employed deception by using camouflage in order to approach and kill easily startled animals such as deer, he also had to learn the art of surprise and use the unexpected as a weapon against stronger enemies and tribes.

Man also had to learn how to be cunning. If creeping up on either an easily startled or dangerous animal was not an option, man the hunter learned how to get the animal in question to come to him instead. The classic tiger trap is a good example of how men used their intelligence to conquer beasts, rather than risk their own lives by stalking an elusive or fierce quarry.

The tiger trap is simply a deep pit covered with a thin roof of straw or long grass, with a goat tied nearby as living bait. All hunters would have to do was wait on a hungry tiger to attack the goat, and then spear it to death once it fell into the pit. Many traps work on this same principle—that it is the hunted which sew the seeds of their own destruction by reaching out for an easy meal or something that is desired, unguarded and in plain view. Traps also work on the principle that something is caught more easily if it is distracted, not concentrating, or is in a state of panic and wishes to run to safety. Traps kill and contain men and animals because they are usually unseen and unexpected.

According to the grouchy philosopher, Thomas Hobbes, modern society was formed mainly because of the fear of the unexpected. He pointed out that the strong may well be able to rule the world, but that they would have to sleep sometime, and in sleep no one can guard against an attack by a weaker individual. Therefore, a "social contract" was reached whereby the weak and strong made a pact to have the peace enforced by a third party, the police and the law, etc., thus replacing an individual's combat ability and serving to keep everyone safe regardless of how weak or strong they were.

However, whilst the social contract works in principle, it often does not protect us when we find ourselves in dangerous situations or locations where the voice of the law cannot be heard. In a crowded bar, for example, where a drunken attacker is intent on causing unwarranted damage to someone's face with a beer glass, or on a blood-soaked battlefield where life has no price. In such positions the use of deception is more useful to protecting oneself than quoting articles from the Geneva Convention.

Camouflage

Taken from the French slang "camoufler," camouflage describes that which disguises something else. Originally used by prehistoric hunters to creep up on their soon to be eaten quarry, camouflage was eventually to become one of the most useful tools in warfare.

Although most armies throughout history have chosen to wear brightly coloured uniforms that express facets of national culture, or to inspire fear by their appearance, there have also been those who adopted camouflage as a military aid. Furthermore, everyday clothing or dress may have, in some cases, been used as camouflage, depending on the terrain in which soldiers or warriors lived.

For example, the Highlanders of Scotland may well have been aided by wearing tartan clothing, tartan being woven together in a pattern exclusive not only to a Clan's identity and geographic location, but also to the colours of the Clan's local flora since local plants were used to dye a tartan's wool. The idea that tartan could have been an aid to warfare is further confirmed by the banning of such, together with bag pipes, after the Highland Jacobites were finally defeated at Culloden in 1746.

Sadly, due to frightfully poor battle orders given by a young and inexperienced commander in chief, the Highlanders made no use whatsoever of their tartan camouflage on that painful day. Nor did they employ their ferocious surprise charge and previously successful guerrilla tactics. Instead, they stood cold and tired on a rainy moor, sword in hand, being shot to bits by the cannons and rifles of the Royal Artillery.

The relative unimportance of camouflage to armies throughout history was obviously due to the weapons that were used on the battlefield. Before the widespread use of guns and accurate field artillery, an army had to rely on cold steel alone. As such, close quarter combat with swords and daggers demands the use of armour rather than a disguise. Camouflage uniforms would only be useful to scouts or spies in reconnaissance missions, or assassins and small ambush units.

However, in modern warfare, in which snipers can shoot an enemy from half a mile away, camouflage is vital for disguising both advancing troops and the position of the sniper himself. Moreover, camouflage has also become advantageous to jungle warfare, where soldiers can exploit a wealth of natural cover, or in desert and arctic warfare, where uniforms can match the exact colour of the area that troops are located.

Although it may seem both helpful and obvious to wear colours found in a surrounding environment, the British army did not begin to wear green as a form of camouflage until 1797, in the 60th Royal American Regiment. Moreover, the British did not wear khaki until 1857, in the 52nd Light Infantry based in India, when the benefits of wearing a uniform the colour of dust/excrement ("khak") were finally realised.

However, the more complicated patterns in camouflage uniforms were not commonly used until WWII, when certain divisions of the German SS started to wear what is commonly known today as Disruptive Pattern Material, composed of natural colours displayed by most European vegetation and soil.

Of course, no one material can provide exact camouflage for every environment, and is therefore subject to constant revision depending on the environment in which an army finds itself. British DPM consists of green and brown splotches reflecting the grassy and muddy hues of the UK countryside, whilst Russian and Austrian camouflage is more of a pattern of autumnal-coloured spots.

American camouflage has had many incarnations, ranging from the tiger stripe pattern used in Vietnam to the desert "chocolate chip" currently used in the Middle East. Modern armies may also employ white camouflage for arctic warfare, and more geometric patterned material for urban combat, with city hues such as blue, grey and black.

Whatever the pattern of camouflage that is chosen, the main point to remember is that in a country environment one's camouflage must appear to be soft and broken rather than straight and hard. This is due to the fact that nature generally has no straight lines. Therefore, a soldier in the field must not only try to adopt a uniform that uses natural colours and patterns, but he must also try to break up the outline of his body.

Indeed, many soldiers use what is known as a "ghillie suit," a device used by gamekeepers and poachers alike in times of peace. Essentially, the string-like material of a ghillie suit is placed over the head and hangs freely over the body, giving the impression of a dark mass, rather than a human appearance. For added effect plants, leaves and grass can be woven into the material.

Although camouflage is something commonly thought of as belonging to a soldier's uniform, it can also be used to disguise anything from a tank to an entire airfield. In the Second World War important runways were painted to look like a patchwork of craters, giving an enemy's aerial reconnaissance the impression that it had been heavily bombed. The camouflage of large areas even went to the extreme of Germany building a false bridge in Hamburg, and disguising the real bridge and on-looking harbour located nearby. The fake bridge thus presented itself as the new and accessible target to allied bombers.

As technology continues to advance, camouflage will become more effective. Perhaps one day it may even be possible to outfit soldiers in chameleon-like uniforms that change colour appropriate to any environment. Moreover, as we continue our modern voyage though the age of high-tech, perhaps it will even be possible to create "cloaking devices" previously found in science fiction, allowing us to simply vanish from the gaze of a camera, radar or the naked eye itself.

Stealth

Although many teenage boys have posters of American-radar-evading stealth bombers on their bedroom walls, they would perhaps be interested to learn that stealth has, in the past, been the weapon of those who did not possess the might and technology of a Superpower. Indeed, stealth is more frequently the favoured weapon of those who have been outnumbered or outgunned by an enemy, and have to rely on guerrilla tactics in order to achieve their military objective.

Throughout history there have been groups or civilisations who were masters of their environment and regarded nature as their ally. The native Indians of North and South America are two of the most respected groups to use stealth to mount attacks or evade capture from invaders. Although better known for their fighting prowess, disciplined training regimes and extremely modest living, the ancient Spartans used stealth on a daily basis in order just to eat.

It was obviously felt by the strict commanders of the day that Spartan soldiers would soon recognise the power of stealth if they were forced to slip past their own night sentries in order to hunt for food outside their camp. Moreover, if any soldier was caught sneaking back into the camp with such food he would be brutally punished. This is harsh training indeed.

Perhaps the most famous shadow warriors to use stealth and deception to their advantage were the Ninja. Inhabiting the mountainous regions of Iga and Koga as far back as the 11th Century, "Shinobi" were the subject of both fear and loathing in feudal Japan. The Shinobi were small communities of people who chose to lead simple lives devoted to spiritual enlightenment. Derived from a religious belief in the five universal elements of earth, water, fire, air (wind) and void (in this case the Zen idea of "nothingness," the unpredictable, the unknown), Ninja were forced to become adept at combat in order to protect their hidden villages from successions of malevolent Shoguns. And so, those who followed the way of Nin: stealth, espionage and invisibility, soon became both an asset to warlords and, at times, their most bitter enemies.

Hired for assassination and spying duties, Ninja were masters of various forms of deception such as make-up and disguise, night manoeuvres, and the use of "magic" or psychic powers. The Ninja also encouraged the superstitious beliefs in Tengu crow demons and evil curses held by peasants to gain a further edge to their unnerving presence. Often sporting scary wooden face masks whilst using fireworks to project flaming missiles into the air, Shinobi inspired stories of gross hyperbole and rumours of their superhuman ability, which is unmatched even by today's standards.

This legacy has been exploited by both the Hollywood and Hong Kong film industries. Yet, unfortunately, films portraying Ninja or today's elite military forces as being invincible can actually be damaging to the appreciation and respect of their legitimate skills. The Spartans, Ninja, Zulus, Apache, British SAS, Russia's Spetsnaz, and America's Delta and Navy SEAL "DEV-GRU" units are all legendary fighters. But no one is invincible. After all, if such fighters were truly invincible they would have no opportunity to express their bravery through combat.

The mythology surrounding a fighter is one thing, the reality something else. SAS troopers, for example, are often portrayed as Rambo look-alikes, shooting people from a mile away, or bursting into houses and causing their enemies to sharply raise their hands in surrender. The reality is that SAS men, when dressed in civilian clothes ("civvies"), look just the same as anyone else. After all, undercover work, off the battlefield, would be pointless if SAS soldiers were spotted instantly due to their "G.I. Joe" and "Action Man" appearance.

The SAS also don't fire hand guns at targets over 20 yards, and are likely to shoot the first person who immediately raises their hands in surrender, being that such a quick reaction indicates reflexes which could also discharge a weapon before they are either restrained or dispatched.

Aside from the Hollywood fiction, the fact is that the Ninja, like today's Special Forces, were expert at using deception in escape, evasion and hand-to-hand combat. Concealed weapons, smoke grenades and eye blinding powders were just some of the many weapons that the exponents of Ninjutsu employed. Furthermore, Ninja psychological warfare was especially concerned with deception as a method of heightening an enemy's fear, and thus unbalancing him mentally as well as physically.

A simple example of this psychological approach could have been demonstrated if a Ninja's opponent confronted him at night. Not only could the Ninja have inspired a great deal of fear by suddenly igniting a firework, producing a sudden ball of light and a loud bang, but it would also have caused a temporary hindrance to night vision. Then, as the opponent stumbled around in the darkness straining his ears to detect the advancing footsteps of the assassin, he would have heard nothing. Silence would have loomed as fear increased. The poor man would no longer have trusted his vision or his sense of hearing, as his imagination ran amok inside his head.

Momentarily blinded and unsure of his surroundings, he would then have been hit once on the face by something unseen. The surprise and shock would have been enough to either send the man running for his life or flailing wildly in defence, until his sense of balance had deserted him.

In this example, all the Ninja had to do was flick a small stone at his enemy, whilst using a complete lack of aggression, and using silence as a psychological weapon. Such combat torpor was, therefore, unexpected, and was a brilliant deception. The Ninja's opponent was beaten because he expected a violent and energetic attack, as the myths surrounding the mountain mystics would have suggested.

Tactics

One of the earliest combat tactics ever to be recorded, the wooden horse of Troy, is also one of the most outstanding forms of deception found in the ancient texts. It is an excellent example of the ingenuity that can be nurtured in times of war. Homer's *Iliad* details several other tactics of deception that were employed by the Greeks to overcome their Trojan foe.

For example, the highly polished breastplate of Achilles was designed not only to enhance his muscular physique, but also to redirect the bright glare of the sun into his opponents' eyes. Indeed, many warriors of old used the sun's reflection off mirror-like armour and shields for this purpose.

The Iliad also details the tactic of feigning retreat. Prior to the wooden horse being dragged into Troy, the Greeks had seemingly abandoned their camps and sailed home in defeat. In reality they had just sailed out of sight, waiting for the signal to return to the fortress city, once its security had been breached by the crafty Odysseus.

In Sun Tzu's masterpiece of strategy, *The Art of War*, the following guidance is offered to warriors of the Orient:

> When able, appear unable
> When employed, appear useless
>
> Lure through advantages
> Take control through confusion
>
> When complete appear to prepare
> When attacked appear separated

Attack when the opponent is unprepared
And appear where least expected.

Sun Tzu's advice would, therefore, seem to encourage the battle tactics of appearing to be in disorder or retreat as a way of luring the enemy into weapon range, or possibly an ambush. Moreover, the expression "a parting shot," meaning to deal a devastating blow as one exits, should actually be "a Parthian shot." The latter version of the expression is named after the Asian horsemen who feigned retreat, before firing arrows back at an enemy that was foolish enough to chase them.

Conversely, instead of pretending a force has retreated or diminished, the deception of making an enemy believe your forces are of greater numbers than they actually are is also one of the oldest combat tactics to be recorded. For example, the Persian emperor Xerxes deliberately let spies and traitors escape from his clutches, to report back to his enemies in northern Greece. The reason for this was that Xerxes' forces were so vast in number that a spy's estimate of their strength would be guaranteed to inspire fear with even a conservative assessment.

Indeed, prior to their defeat at the battle of Thermopylae, the foot soldiers and cavalry of the Persian army were thought to be in their millions. However, a more realistic number is actually around 30,000 men, many of whom were peasants that Xerxes had forcefully drafted into to his army from villages and towns that he had passed through and ultimately defeated on the long march to Greece.

Once in Greece, Xerxes again disguised the true number of his troops, but this time it was of the dead. The Persian emperor ordered that 19,000 of the 20,000 of his slain men be buried immediately, so as the corpses would not dishearten the remaining Persians and remind them of the futility of their disastrous campaign.

Modern warfare also has many instances of troop numbers being overestimated by an enemy. The Falklands War has the example of soldiers from Britain's Parachute Regiment forcing an Argentinean detachment to surrender by bombarding their position with a devastating show of strength. In a risky move, the Paras used up most of their ammunition in the space of 24 hours instead of conserving bullets and mortar shells, a necessity of airborne infantry troops.

However, such was the ferocity of their attack that the heat generated by the hail of constant bullets was so great that it set the entire hillside on fire, thus leaving the Argentineans no choice but to surrender, lest they be burnt alive or shot to pieces. The Argentineans who were subsequently captured honestly believed they had been under attack by Britain's main artillery, rather than the small but deadly spearhead of the infantry.

Although this was an instance where deception was used as the best weapon in the circumstances, the award for using deception as the main weapon has to go to one of the most respected commanders in modern warfare, the soldier's soldier, Erwin Rommel. Fronting Hitler's Afrika Korps throughout WWII, Rommel was so adept at detecting and evading allied traps that he was nick-named "the Desert Fox."

The fear inspired by Rommel's presence was so great that allied forces that were stationed in North Africa had to be constantly reminded that he was just a clever tactician, and was not in possession of occult powers. This was a view that many of his defeated opponents found very difficult to accept.

Believing that "an admiral never won a battle from port," Erwin Rommel was with his troops constantly, giving him the ability to act quickly and make rapid changes to his army's position and daily battle orders.

During the North African campaign Rommel is especially remembered for two instances in particular that show his true mastery of deception. Knowing there to be many foreign enemy agents working out of Tripoli, Rommel decided to give spies something to report when he told the Afrika Korps to drive their armoured vehicles through the city several times in succession. This circular stream of vehicles passing through the city again and again, thus gave the impression that the Nazi forces were of greater numbers than they actually were.

Furthermore, when on the move, Rommel would insist his troops used anything with an engine and wheels to belt across the desert at high speed. The more vehicles the better, as the resulting cloud of dust, which could be seen from many miles away, would serve to give the impression of a powerful force in rapid advance to battle.

Aside from perverting Allied estimates of his force's strength and position, Rommel also used deception to cover his initial lack of tanks and armoured cars at the start of the desert campaign. Instructing carpenters to build wooden turrets and guns, the Nazi commander ordered that they be mounted on the roofs of Volkswagens, therefore giving Allied aerial reconnaissance the chance to take pictures of tanks and APCs long before a single Panzer arrived in Africa.

However, the use of dummy guns and tanks was not exclusive to the Afrika Korps. The Second World War saw a vast selection of mock tanks, trains, aircraft, buildings and even airfields being created by both German and allied forces. Moreover, a special unit of the SS didn't exist at all, and was only present as a ghost army of papier-maché soldiers, left in abandoned positions to keep the advance of allied soldiers at bay. Yet such dummy armies are by no means the exclusive property of WWII. Modern decoy tanks, for example, come complete with heating elements inside their cardboard shell, giving the appearance of a hot engine and a human presence inside.

Close Quarter Combat

The use of deception when having a close quarter fight with an opponent can certainly help to turn the situation to your advantage. Whether it be the crude use of sucker punches or more complicated character-acting in order to gain a moment's sympathy or promote fear in an enemy's heart, a lie may just save your life.

Ancient Japan's "sword saint," Miyamoto Musashi, described several ways to win a battle by using deception in his masterpiece, *Book of Five Rings*, a brilliant piece of literature that is even now used by both businessmen and practitioners of Kenjutsu alike. Musashi's unique use of deception is that he uses a wooden sword to lull his opponents into a false sense of security. Unfortunately for them, Musashi then, with the sun in the eyes of his enemies, smashes their skulls quite effectively with his wooden sword, and without the need for a tempered steel blade.

Another interesting deception detailed by Musashi is of feigning sickness or tiredness as a way to get an opponent to drop his guard, or as the sword saint put it, to become infected by sleep and apathy. Musashi is not saying that an opponent will give up his attack if he thinks he has the advantage, he is rather suggesting that an attacker will concentrate his energy on the final killing blow and disregard further defensive manoeuvres.

Therefore, if applied to business, a rival company may well claim public victory over your own firm before the end game proper has even been reached. However, if your company was feigning injury or defeat, and suddenly found new strength in a hidden financial investment, the rival firm, now without its boasts of certain victory, may lose the confidence of share holders and face potential boardroom sackings.

Although Musashi's work can today be employed in business, as can both Sun Tzu's and Machiavelli's *Art Of War*, their original purpose was to educate commanders either in close quarter combat or large scale battle techniques. In modern times, however, it has been Bruce Lee whom has had the most influence in the world of martial arts, whilst military close combat fighting techniques have been influenced by war heroes such as Fairbairn, Sykes, Drexel Biddle and Applegate.

The difference in these approaches to close quarter combat is that Bruce Lee was an expert in self defence for civilians in domestic situations, whilst Fairbairn and Drexel Biddle specialised in the science of killing enemy soldiers in the theatre of war.

As cinema icon, fighter and philosopher, it was Bruce Lee who recommended that we should "absorb what is useful," a statement coming from his observation of worthless or superfluous techniques that hinder martial artists rather than assist them. Striving to preserve the best techniques from all combat arts, Lee invented his own eclectic style known as "Jeet Kune Do," or "the Way of the Intercepting Fist," a name that Lee himself regretted, as a name implies limitation. If an art has a name, it can be known, and its style and response to an attack predicted. Lee wanted something without limitation or predictability.

Being that the martial arts were created to help individuals defend themselves against stronger foes, and also to increase the effectiveness of soldiers in hand-to-hand combat, deception is a central pillar of such arts. Classical forms of Kung-Fu, for example, use various animal styles such as "Monkey" and "Praying Mantis," which employ a myriad of deceptive movements and stances. These stances encourage an enemy to attack in a certain way, and therefore be controlled by the defender, who can hopefully predict the attacker's strategy. A practitioner of Monkey Kung Fu will also leap, tumble, twist and turn, all in order to fool and confuse an attacker. Furthermore, classical martial arts weapons, such as the fan and tasselled spear, are used to distract an opponent's attention before an unexpected strike is delivered.

Martial Arts in general use a vast range of techniques that throw an opponent's attention in the opposite direction from a defender's blow, thus making an attacker's own defence difficult. We could point and look upwards, an attacker may then look up, and hopefully miss the kick we then deliver to his knee.

Essentially the philosophy behind combat misdirection has the aim of making an opponent think you are about to do one thing, before doing something else, deliberately telegraphing your intention to throw a big "haymaker" punch to an enemy's head, but actually punching him in the gut. Or waving your hand in an opponent's face to concentrate his attention, before quickly dropping down on one knee to deliver a devastating punch to his groin.

Sucker punch techniques go even further than conventional martial arts deception, in that the use of acting is often employed to set up the sucker punch. An example of this could be Musashi's feigning injury ploy, where you are punched in the gut and make a big deal of it, panting, crying and groaning in mock agony. But whilst you are bent over in apparent distress and unable to breath, you can either stand up quickly to catch your opponent's chin or nose with the back of your head, or turn around to deliver a swift back-kick or other quick attack.

Following the idea that the first person to strike unexpectedly in a fight has a good chance of ending the fight as the victor, we could even go down the path of what could be termed "dirty tricks." Fighting dirty is a pretty meaningless term, however, as there are no "clean" fights on the street or battlefield. All is fair in love and war!

A dirty trick could arise when you predict a fight will shortly take place. Perhaps an ex-boyfriend of your partner is drunk, jealous and arguing with you in a bar. He is aggressive and really seems to be keen on a fight. Perhaps he is bigger than you and handy with his fists. The only advantage you have is, therefore, by viciously attacking him when he is unguarded and unprepared for your strike.

So, offer him a cigarette or ask him a crazy and off-the-wall question to briefly take his mind off his own plan of attack.

"C'mon have a cigarette. Hey, did you hear about the free cars they're giving away downtown?"

Either puffing on a cigarette or asking more details about the free cars, your opponent's mouth will be open and his jaw muscles will be relaxed. This is the perfect moment to hit him in the mouth with a strong and unmercifully violent punch, hopefully breaking his jaw with ease and bringing an immediate close to the fight, essentially before it began.

The cigarette sucker punch has an additional barb if your opponent has facial hair. Kindly light up his cigarette, then set fire to his beard and punch him in the face. As he excitedly pats out the fire on his face he'll also be adding to the pain of his broken nose.

If you regard this last scenario as brutal, savage and distasteful then you are quite correct. As the fictional soldier Rambo once said, "In order to survive a war you have to become war." If a mugger, rapist, junkie, skinhead thug or other violent attacker tries to assault or kill you or your family, being civilised will hinder your chances of survival. If you just stand still, defecate in your trousers, scream or cry, your attacker will see your reaction as a sign of weakness and complete unwillingness to defend yourself. He will exploit this weakness and make you suffer for it.

Fight or flight, defend yourself or run away.

Martial Arts

As previously mentioned, martial artists use a treasure trove of deception to fool opponents and win a fight. However, aside from the deception employed in their combat techniques and attacks, martial artists are sometimes guilty of quite another deception altogether. This is the deception of feigning superior ability and possession of secret knowledge in order to procure movie roles and book deals, and make a vast amount of money from teaching their naïve students.

At the end of the Second World War many American and British servicemen returned home with tales of amazing feats performed by martial artists in Japan, Okinawa and Southeast Asia. The interest in arts such as Judo, Karate and Jui-Jitsu grew until martial arts classes sprang up all over America, Europe and Australia. The wave of global interest in the martial arts continued through the fifties, sixties and seventies, and eventually included other arts such as Kung Fu, Kempo, Tae Kwon Do, Kendo and Aikido. In more recent years even more "exotic" arts were included to the list, including Kali, Escrima, Arnis, Jeet Kune Do, Thai Boxing, Silat, Hapkido, Tang Soo Do, Savate, Budo, Russian Systema and Ninjutsu.

Over the last two decades it has been Ninjutsu that has proven to be one of the largest producers of fraudulent "Masters" and "Grandmasters" of various styles and schools, previously unheard of by the majority of martial arts practitioners. Cashing-in on the "Ninja boom" that began in the 1980s, various con-men have, for years, made a small fortune by telling us that they are "the world's most dangerous fighter" and the sole keeper of the forbidden "Ninja magic" or "Dim Mak death touch" secrets. Supposedly, these secrets hold the key to a deadly touch that could instantly cause an opponent's heart to explode, or begin a physiological chain reaction that would result in a victim's death several days later—techniques that would give Mr. Spock from "Star Trek" a run for his money.

One of the most famous of the "world's deadliest man" camp of charlatans was John Keehan, a 1970s hairdresser who co-founded the United States Karate Association. Bored with his regular status of being a decidedly average Karate exponent, Keehan changed his name to "Count Dante" and founded The Black Dragon Fighting Society. Dante claimed to be the winner of a tournament called The World's Overall Fighting Championship, where he defeated experts in Kung Fu, Karate, Judo and Aikido, experts who have unsurprisingly never come forward to verify Dante's story.

It was through the Black Dragon Fighting Society, and children's comic books, that Dante advertised himself as the "deadliest man alive," and sold his Dim Mak guidebook to teenagers and gullible weaklings around the world. The book, described as "horrifyingly dangerous and brutally vicious," promised that those who master the "dance of death" would be invincible fighters. And also, I assume, unwelcome at a disco. The book also came with a $10,000 dollar guarantee that it was "deadlier" than anything ever written, and that readers could break bricks with their bare hands after only a few minutes of training.

Dante's premise for the book was that he had acquired "terrifying" skills from a secret Oriental fighting society, including the "77 poison hand" technique that can "maim, disfigure, cripple or kill," but was willing to share his knowledge at great personal risk, for only $5.50 including postage.

Count Dante died of a bleeding ulcer in 1975, or perhaps he was the victim of a secret and deadly Saturday night fever, or a boogieing Bee-Gees Ninja who had mastered the funky Dim Mak dance. Dante obviously had trouble staying alive!

Perhaps inspired by Dante's quest for fame and his money-making scams, two notorious "Ninjas" whom we should be aware of are "Supreme Grandmaster" Ashida Kim and "Grandmaster" Frank Dux. Kim is the author of books and the star of training DVDs on the subject of "Ninjitsu," with titles such as "Ninja Death Touch," "Ninja Secrets of Invisibility," "Ninja Mind Control" and "How To Be A Ninja." However, his credentials for being a Ninja himself are as invisible as the skills he purports to teach. Mr. Kim (a.k.a. Radford W. Davis or Christopher Hunter) has not yet managed to convince the martial arts community that he is anything more that a Karate exponent with delusions of grandeur.

Kim, in his defence, has issued a challenge to anyone brave enough to face him. He has stated that he will prove to all those who doubt his amazing talent, and that if he is defeated by them in a fight, they can keep his $10,000 appearance fee. However, aside from having to fork out a $10,000 appearance fee, challengers also have to pay an additional $25,000 to cover Kim's travel, accommodation and legal expenses. Kim stipulates that the fight will be decided in his favour if the challenger commits an "unsportsmanlike act," or places his shoulders on the ground for more than five seconds.

I'd like to ask Mr. Kim what he views as unsportsmanlike in a fight. A punch, a kick, a choke... what? After all, the real art of Ninjutsu is, itself, not regarded as being very sporting. It is a deadly art that aims to hurt, maim or kill a violent attacker. Moreover, if Mr. Kim was able to turn himself invisible and use powerful mind control techniques on his enemies, why would he be so unwilling to fight them? Ninjas aren't afraid to kill, are they, Mr. Kim?

After you have watched an Ashida Kim Ninja training DVD or read a few chapters of one of his books, you may ask yourself why he calls himself a "Supreme Grandmaster." Skulking around in black pyjamas with a sword is something a teenager may do in his bedroom, but serious students of the martial arts should find Kim's "Ninjitsu" instruction to be entirely fraudulent.

Kim's books are a treat. Why don't you invest in "Ninja Levitation" and learn to fly? Cut down on airline ticket costs next time you want a holiday abroad. Or read *Way of the Spider* and learn to "sting" your enemies. Nobody has told Kim that a spider doesn't sting, it bites.

Other great Kim titles are *Cloak of Invisibility*, where fearful Ninjas can hide under their safety blanket. Or Kim's masterpiece, *The Invisible Fist of the Ninja*, which has a cover photo of Kim posing in yellow pyjamas and wearing a ludicrous bone facemask. In this book the reader will find the forbidden secrets of breathing fire like a dragon.

The supreme grandmaster of black pyjamas has also broken into the soft-core pornography market by penning an erotic novel, *The Amorous Adventures of Ashida Kim*. The book details Kim's time in Africa as a secret agent posing as a brothel bouncer. Kim not only claims that he has taught CIA agents, but also that he has worked as a secret agent himself.

Do yourself a favour, go online and look to the web site of "Dojo Press." Not only will you find Ashida Kim titles, you will also discover a bounty of bullshit; for instance, books such as *Kato San*, an executive security training manual that sounds like it was written for the fictional "Kato" character in "The Green Hornet," played by Bruce Lee. However, in all actuality it should probably should be read by the fictional "Kato" character in the Pink Panther comedy movies.

Another "Ninja" and "CIA agent" with whom we should familiarise ourselves is an American Karate instructor called Frank Dux. Dux allegedly makes many wild claims, including the idea that he was a highly decorated Vietnam veteran, that he can break bullet proof glass with a punch, that he holds records for kicking speed, that he knocked out around sixty men in a single fight, and that he is a Ninja grandmaster.

Dux claims to have been taught a secret style of Ninjutsu in Japan, and was the winner of what he refers to as "The Kumite," or a fight to the death using any style or technique. In actuality, the Japanese term "kumite" means nothing of the kind, and just refers to the act of practise sparring.

In the 1980s, many members of the international martial arts community were impressed with Dux's claims, and this new-found fame even led to Dux being the inspiration for "Bloodsport," a kickboxing movie starring Jean Claude Van Damme. A movie that drew parallel scenes from "Enter the Dragon" and "The Octagon," "Bloodsport" detailed the story of how Dux won the Kumite death match. "Bloodsport" may also have inspired Mixed Martial Arts (MMA) ultimate cage fighting, popularised by Brazilian Jui-Jitsu and kickboxing practitioners today. The honour may also fall on Count Dante's shoulders, with his World's Overall Fighting Championship.

As is the case with those who claim to be grandmasters, or the highest ranked expert and patron of a particular style of martial arts, all it takes is for one to observe the so-called grandmaster in action, and draw their own conclusions. Anyone who has seen Dux in action may realise that, far from being an expert in Ninjutsu, he simply uses basic Karate moves and stances that are entirely unrelated to the aforementioned art.

It seems Mr. Dux has performed the greatest of a Ninja's tricks, by becoming invisible. He no longer enjoys his "legendary" status, and was last seen in court when he attempted to sue Jean Claude Van Damme for over a million dollars. Dux claimed Van Damme stole his idea for a movie titled "The Quest," which, in reality, was more like a 1979 movie called "The Silent Flute" (a.k.a. "The Circle of Iron"), written in part by Bruce Lee, and was also similar to "Raiders of the Lost Ark."

Those interested in learning a martial art should do some research before committing to a class or paying course fees. Go and watch a few lessons at different martial arts dojos or training halls. Don't settle for bullshit because you are afraid of telling a master that his techniques are rotten. Don't be impressed by martial arts certificates or black belts. Anyone who is computer literate can print off an authentic looking certificate saying they are a grandmaster, and anyone can buy a black belt at a sports equipment store.

The King of rock n' roll, Elvis Presley, told people he was a thirteenth Dan grade in his funky Memphis style of Karate. I'm certain Elvis was competent in the art, but to say that one is so highly graded is a joke. An exceptionally skilled master of the martial arts, at the very top of his game, should have around a four to nine Dan black belt grade.

Yet people who don't understand the martial arts, or who want to con others, view black belts and Dan grades as something to hold in awe. But it should be remembered that a deadly street fighter may not have a black belt at all. Indeed, as Mr. Miyagi said in "The Karate Kid," "Karate here [mind], Karate here [heart], Karate never here [belt]."

In the martial arts, verification of credentials and qualifications is quite difficult, and the old saying "actions speak louder than words" is appropriate when deciding on the ability and knowledge of a practitioner, teacher, master or grandmaster.

So many Westerners have travelled to China and Japan to sign up for a month-long class with some a dime-a-dozen grandmaster of some phoney baloney style of Kung Fu or Ninjutsu, simply to get a certificate and return home to write a series of books. However, when one examines the information contained in such books, or attends an instant-master's class, it is quickly recognised that the martial arts "expert" and author is nothing of the sort.

In China anyone can say they are a master or grandmaster of Kung Fu, justifying their claim by saying they practise a style only their family knows, or that they were the secret student of a famous grandmaster. A poor, unemployed man in China can easily make money by saying that he is an ex-Shaolin monk or a Kung Fu master, especially if they teach rich Westerners who are desperate to learn an exotic Oriental art so that they can, themselves, teach it back home, and make a fortune doing so.

Two such dubious "Grandmasters" are William Cheung and Leung Ting, both of whom say they were "closed door" students of the late Grandmaster of Wing Chun Kung Fu, Yip Man, a master who was Bruce Lee's genuine teacher. The term "closed door" implies that they were taught things the other students were not.

Both Cheung and Ting have dragged the style of Wing Chun (a.k.a. Ving Tsun and Wing Tzun) through the mud over the years, each bickering over who had greater seniority and who is really Yip Man's heir. Whilst old photographs of Ting have proven he was not as senior a student as he suggests, the most compelling evidence of the lack of grandmaster status comes with a short video clip of William Cheung.

The old clip, which can be seen on YouTube, shows Cheung giving a Wing Chun demonstration class at a seminar in Germany. As Cheung talks to his students he is suddenly attacked by Emin Boztepe, a Turkish martial artist who doubted Cheung's ability. The short fight turns to farce when Cheung offers no resistance and is swept to the ground by Boztepe, who sits on Cheung's chest and punches him in the face until he is dragged off by shocked onlookers.

Cheung and Ting are best-selling authors of Wing Chun instructional books, no doubt due to the connection they had to Yip Man, and therefore also with Bruce Lee.

When it comes to the instructional DVD or book market, those who purchase such wares should be cautious about spending too much money. When I lived in China I bought a few cheap DVDs claiming to show instruction on Bruce Lee's Jeet Kune Do style. However, when I played these DVDs I discovered a frail Chinese gentleman dressed in Tai Chi garb, showing pictures of Bruce Lee (which were torn from a magazine), whilst telling viewers how to breath properly and that they should buy his other DVDs.

People are attracted by the idea of a quick way to end a fight, as most of us are not hard, muscular fighters with skill, speed and stamina. Therefore, when someone comes along and says they have the ability to end a fight with no need to even touch an opponent, public interest is automatically guaranteed.

Harry Thomas "Tom" Cameron, an obese American martial arts instructor nicknamed "the human stun gun," was once the subject of a FOX-News report. The TV report showed Cameron magically waving his hands in front of his terrified and equally overweight students, causing them all to collapse on the ground. Of course, the outcome of his magic motions was not repeated when FOX-News took Cameron to a Jui-Jitsu Dojo, where genuine martial artists were completely unmoved and unimpressed.

Cameron explained that the men he faced in the Jui-Jitsu Dojo were not susceptible to his subtle Dim Mak gestures as they were trained fighters who could resist the effects of energy attacks. Well fancy that, trained fighters don't fall down when someone waves their hands in front of their face. What does Mr. Cameron think a street thug would do? What type of self defence is he offering when he has to tell his opponent "I'm going to send energy towards you and you may faint and collapse"? Maybe attackers would indeed collapse if they were told this, but only in fits of laughter!

The technique of telling someone what they are about to do, and how people are supposed to react, is often used by stage hypnotists and TV evangelists. The "power of suggestion" in some way overrides the will of weak minded individuals who want to be dominated and controlled by a person with a stronger personality. Indeed, if a person is nervous and is being watched by a crowd of people, to suddenly be struck on the neck or head may cause them to stumble backwards, giving the appearance of fainting.

Moreover, who is really going to admit, in front of a large audience or devotees of a martial arts guru, that actually they don't feel moved at all?

Most of us will play along and pretend to be struck by an unseen force, rather than risk the embarrassment caused by arguing with the master, evangelist or hypnotist and calling their bluff. Others simply want to believe, so they do believe.

"Yes, it was amazing. I could actually feel the force of his blow hitting my stomach from the other side of the room."

Bullshit! It was probably just indigestion from eating all those burgers for lunch, you weak-minded lard-ass! What does it say to you when a master can knock out his students, but not a "real person" whom he doesn't know? You should tell yourself that the master is a con man, with sycophantic and fearful students who don't wish to upset the man whom they pay handsomely for classes every week.

Of course, the other answer to why students of Cameron are willing to collapse so easily in front of TV cameras or newspaper reporters, is that some people love fame and attention at any cost. Like the sad lonely man who allows himself to be thrown "by the unseen hand of God" whenever a charismatic Evangelist calls him up on stage. Moreover, I suggest that many of Cameron's students are collaborators in the con.

Take, for example, Cameron's appearance on the TV show "Steve Harvey's Big Time," an upbeat vehicle for music and guest appearances, which is aimed at the Black African-American audience. As a novelty guest on this show, Mr. Cameron was seen to knock out a student, perform a trick of leverage and weight distribution that prevented him from being thrown by the show's host, and finally give a demonstration of his powers on an audience member. The volunteer went down easily and Cameron's students crowded around the unconscious man, flapping air and excitedly commenting that he could have died in twenty seconds if they hadn't resuscitated him.

Bullshit! The entire audience was black, apart from two fat white nerds sitting in the front row, who looked extremely similar to Cameron's cheeseburger-munching white students; fat white nerds who made a big song and dance about wanting to participate and who were eventually chosen to join Cameron on stage. The demonstration was bullshit from start to finish!

Aside from all the stage evangelism "invisible force" baloney, visitors to Cameron's Dim Mak death touch dojo are treated to displays of concrete blocks being broken on his chest with a sledge hammer, whilst he lies on a bed of nails. This trick goes back centuries and can be found throughout India and China as a way in which wandering martial arts street entertainers make money from a gullible audience.

Cameron, "the human stun gun," is a student of an even more controversial figure, so called "Grandmaster" George Dillman, a Karate instructor who claimed in a National Geographic documentary that he taught Bruce Lee and Mohammad Ali how to fight. A martial artist who says he has "flat-lined several people" and that he can knock down the world's biggest man with one finger. The secret to Dillman's ability lies in his use of pressure-point strikes and manipulation of "chi," the mysterious energy that most martial artists are taught to harness, and yet which remains unexplained by science.

Dillman claims he can knock someone out without touching them, simply by throwing a ball of invisible energy at them—a technique he claims to successfully use to move lines of people standing in front of him in a queue at Starbucks.

However, Dillman also explains that his "no touch knock out" can be countered and "nullified" if an opponent wiggles his tongue or raises his big toes. I suggest, therefore, that those students who fork out large sums of money to learn Dillman's magical moves, tell an attacker not to speak or move his feet. Otherwise, their non-existent self defence techniques will be nullified along with their bank balance.

The last alleged charlatan whom I want to mention is American Dr. John M. La Tourrette, 10th degree "Grandmaster" of Dim Mak and speed hitting. Mr. Tourettee says he is "the nation's leading expert on mind training, for martial arts" and is famous for his rapid combination attacks.

However, this master's pitiful displays of speedy self-defence techniques are more amusing than the Bible's book of Genesis, and far more tragic. Anyone who imagines a heavy, muscular and violent attacker will be knocked down by silly, flowery, flapping chops and slaps is kidding themselves.

Speed is an asset in the martial arts, but should not be relied upon as a sole defence. There has to be some strength, some force and some power applied to one's punches in order to make them effective. Also, you may notice that martial arts fraudsters who use very quick flurries of punches never seem to direct them at a particular target and, as such, their demonstration will seem inept and chaotic to those who know how to fight.

For example, mimicking Bruce Lee in one of his movies, and erupting in a rapid attack of fifty strikes to a willing guinea pig's torso, may impress a group of sniggering schoolgirls, but it won't impress a Thai boxer. A Thai boxer knows that if he hits someone around the shoulders, back and upper arm a hundred times, he would just be wasting time and energy. Speed is only as asset if a punch is aimed at a weak or vulnerable point of the body.

Let me remind you that it is unusual in a real fight for an opponent to simply stand still and allow themselves to be punched fifty times without moving away or blocking the punches. Indeed, if you see a Tae Kwon Do man kicking a training partner twenty times on the head, whilst the partner stands still with his arms at his side, ask yourself on what planet such a fight would ever take place. Tip: if you try to kick someone more than twice in the head, chances are they'll reach out, grab your leg, push you to the ground, and own your ass right there!

Accompanied by mouthed "fhew fhew" sound effects that he makes while demonstrating his skills, the speed grandmaster Tourrette entitles his sissy punches to an opponent's head as, "a straight angle hit, to the high sectional concept of the upper quadrant." For Christ's sake, since when is a punch on the nose a f***ing "concept"? I suggest Dr. Dim Mak needs a swift kick to his straight angle, low sectional concept, and a hundred-punch flurry to his quadrant!

Another tip: if you hear someone waffling on about "concepts" and using pseudo-scientific technical jargon to describe something that can be explained in simple language, chances are they're talking crap.

Martial arts charlatans and fraudsters are plentiful, but there is one piece of advice that should protect anyone from becoming the student of a fake grandmaster. Don't look for "secret" techniques, "death touches," "energy blows," or a style, stance or technique that someone claims will make a practitioner invincible. Also, be cautious of martial arts masters who charge a fortune because they have some distant and dubious link to Bruce Lee. Many people met Bruce Lee and have been photographed standing next to him. But standing next to Lee doesn't make them any more qualified to teach martial arts.

And if you don't believe me I'll use my secret Ninja invisible finger magic energy death ray on you, Bzzzzzzzzzz!! Do you feel that high sectional concept working? Bzzzzzzzzzzzzz!! You are feeling drowsy. You are in my power, Bzzzzzzzzzzzz!!

No, perhaps not.

Special Operations

Be it espionage, infiltration behind enemy lines, or the science of cryptography and stenography, special operations are entirely synonymous with deception.

Although Hollywood has helped to nurture the stereotypical image of gadget-encrusted spies, special forces and intelligence personnel who are armed with a plethora of weird and wonderful equipment, the reality of special operations and espionage is even stranger than the myth.

Although films concerning the exploits of the charismatic yet fictional James Bond help to maintain the highly competent image of Britain's intelligence services, Bond's quartermaster mentor "Q" would certainly belong to the world of fact. Now free from the restraints of the Official Secrets Act, a catalogue detailing British Special Operations Executive equipment has been released that makes amusing reading. Indeed, any catalogue of equipment from agencies such as the SOE, CIA, MI6 or KGB is amusing, fascinating and unnerving to boot. If necessity is the mother of invention, global espionage has many dangerous and deceptive children.

Such James Bond gadgets may include cigarette-lighter recording devices, minute cameras, concealed radio transmitters and a myriad of exotic weapons such as umbrella rifles, coin knives and pen guns.

Two of the more bizarre SOE gadgets are mock camel dung and fake rats, which were used to disguise anti-personnel mines, planted by agents on North African roads used by the Nazis in WWII. The American Office of Strategic Services (OSS) was also notorious for their clever use of such ingenious gadgetry, used for espionage and escape from enemy hands.

Aside from mines, booby traps are key to an operative's mastery of sabotage. However, it is not so much the mechanics of assembling such traps that is important, but rather an agent's ability to disguise the trap to avoid its discovery. For example, in past wars the soldiers who planted neat rows of mines over large fields were often disappointed when the whole area was avoided by the enemy, even if only one of the planted mines had been discovered.

However, when explosive booby traps were attached to apparently abandoned equipment such as guns, ammunition, water canteens or food, the enemy was constantly tempted to approach such bait, and therefore constantly risking their lives. Essentially, booby traps do not have to be overly sophisticated or high-tech, they simply need to be well placed to avoid suspicion and detection.

Why bother setting up a complicated infra-red detonation trigger when a clothes peg and wire can do the same job? What is the point of fashioning a clever time bomb when a light-bulb filled with volatile material would be ignited by the target's finger pressing on a darkened room's light switch?

It is not only behind-the-lines equipment and booby traps that are useful to intelligence or sabotage operations. Deception carried in radio broadcasts, filling the airwaves with misinformation and propaganda, is also a useful tool in times of war.

Middle Eastern agencies who wage war with Western countries have often found a great deal of success in the misinformation trick. However, the best examples of war propaganda and misinformation were seen in WW II. Both allied and axis propaganda agencies broadcast misleading information to opposing forces (allied to axis, axis to allied). The troops who listened to their enemy's radio broadcasts were told that their wives would be raped if they did not return home to protect them, and that the entire war effort was a waste of time and to simply stop fighting.

Perhaps one of the most outrageous misinformation scams of modern warfare, aside from "Monty's Double," was WW II's "Operation Mincemeat." This naval intelligence initiative essentially employed the services of a Scottish man, whom had died from pneumonia, as a floating carrier of misinformation, inside a German controlled area of the Mediterranean.

The corpse, which was dressed as an officer in the Royal Marines, was given the identity of Major Martin, along with fake love letters from his imaginary girlfriend and a folder of information about an apparent allied attack on Greece, "Operation Husky." Of course, the deception was that the officer had drowned whilst attempting to deliver the top-secret documents, intended to lead German troops to Greece from their base in Sicily, the real target of a British invasion.

Although the world of special operations seems to use deception at every opportunity, it is unfortunate that the same knowledge is now available to those who would use such deception against civilised countries to promote terrorism. A false identity and background history may help an intelligence agent gain access to terrorist cells, but fake IDs can also allow terrorists to enter countries where an attack on innocent people is planned.

After September 11th, aircraft security was stepped up, especially with regard to the confiscation of bladed items and liquids. However, deceptive weapons such as glass-reinforced nylon daggers could now be used in air terrorism, being that such weapons, apart from having their blades being concealed inside everyday items such as hair-brush handles or rulers, etc., can evade detection from metal detectors. Furthermore, perhaps the greatest deception employed by terrorists or spies is the need to carry such weapons as knives in the first place. This, of course, makes security procedures at airports and ship ports a complete red herring, as it is the terrorist himself who is the lethal weapon, not the knives and bombs that he is expected to carry!

There is really no need for James-Bond-style concealed weapons, as professional killers can use almost anything in existence as an improvised weapon, and would not jeopardise a mission by risking being caught with a gun or a blade on their person. For example, by using elements comprised from certain duty free goods, toiletries and alcoholic beverages sold on board commercial airliners, a sabotage expert could fashion an improvised, timed incendiary device. All that is required is a basic knowledge of electronics and chemistry, and a good imagination.

Moreover, a terrorist who is determined to cause harm to an aircraft cabin crew could, for example, use his shoelaces as a garrotte or a broken mirror or smashed aftershave bottle as a knife. He could stab passengers with a pen used as a mini spear, or even use his bare hands to choke a stewardess to death or break her neck with a karate chop. Security precautions are made even more complicated by the additional hazard of suicidal fanatics, whose presence makes protecting aircraft from attack virtually impossible.

Furthermore, terrorists do not even need to be on board the plane that they wish to sabotage, nor do they need a bomb to cause it to crash. All a clever terrorist needs to do is to get a job in an airline ground crew and gain constant access to a plane's cargo hold, loading and offloading luggage.

All he then has to do, at least hypothetically, is sneak the odd container of mercury on board the plane, and empty it inside. The mercury, being a liquid metal, will run through cracks and spaces inside the aircraft and begin to corrode any aluminium surface. If enough mercury is deposited inside the plane, it may even eat its way through the fuselage, and perhaps cause an unexplainable "accident."

Moreover, the terrorist with a good knowledge of chemistry principles can gain access to an area where he can cause a vast loss of life by simply using the volatile substances and combustible materials he finds around him. Say, for example, a cruise ship is targeted by an extremist group. Cruise ships having thousands of people on board, who terrorists may just be aching to kill, and they carry many thousands of capitalist dollars which I'm sure terrorists would love to destroy. Indeed, a cruise ship is a mighty symbol of capitalist decadence, and is a floating tribute to the luxury, wealth and freedom which Westerners enjoy.

Thus, cruise ships are obvious targets for those who would like to see us all chained to a life of monotonous subservience to a totalitarian state, with severe restrictions on what we can say and even think.

"Filthy imperialist infidels," a bitter terrorist may grumble. "Why should they enjoy a nice relaxing cruise, sipping cocktails, whilst I have to work to sell this shipment of heroin and make some new weapons of mass destruction?"

Religious terrorists must loath the idea of a cruise ship!

The worrying thing is that destroying a cruise ship may be easier that you imagined. All a terrorist would have to do is get a job as an engineering officer, or more realistically, as a simple "motor man" who has access to the ships' massive engine room. Here, in the bowels of the ship, he would find a huge amount and variety of chemicals such as concentrated sulphuric acid and chlorine, or inflammable liquids and highly combustible substances. If a terrorist mixed a strong base with a strong acid he could potentially blow a large hole in the ship's hull, or produce toxic gases which could be sucked into the air vents and throughout the ship.

However, even as a general member of a ships' crew, or perhaps as just a simple passenger, a terrorist on board a cruise ship could quite easily bring death to thousands by resorting to the basic principles of arson. Pick the right moment and ignite as many flammable materials as possible in as many unsupervised areas as possible. Between the hours of 2 AM and 4 AM there is generally only a skeleton staff of officers on a cruise ship who are awake and in charge. At this time, most officers are tired, busy, hung-over, and are certainly not scouting the ship for suspicious passengers carrying a box of matches. Most of the other passengers and crew are sleeping and there is just not enough security staff employed to ensure that closed circuit cameras are monitored 24 hours a day.

Moreover, unlike an aircraft which is put on autopilot for most of a long-haul flight, and has at least one pilot present in the cockpit throughout, a cruise ship may find its bridge completely deserted at times, save for a lowly Asian crewman with a pair of binoculars. Aside from coming into port and sailing out of a busy harbour, cruise ships basically steer themselves, as they are guided by a pre-set course programmed into the navigation computer. So, having a captain and officers present on the bridge at all times is simply not necessary, although it would be reassuring to passengers.

The point I'm making is that a cruise ship could be a soft target for terrorists as there are a very limited amount of things officers, crew, and even passengers could do to thwart and prevent a terrorist attack.

A terrorist may not blow up a ship, but he may want to sink it, and the easiest way to do that is to cause a large and devastating fire to break out. If this fire is allowed to reach the engine room, there will be enough violent explosions to bring tears of joy to a terrorist's lifeless, malevolent, eyes.

Unfortunately there are simply not enough trained officers and crew to effectively attend to more than two large fires on board a ship at the same time. Indeed, it only takes one large fire to spread to the whole vessel and prove disastrous before the order to abandon ship is given.

Although a modern cruise ship is equipped with highly sensitive fire detection and extinguishing devices, fire alarms which alert officers on the ship's bridge to a potential problem are often ignored as they are assumed to be caused by heat surges in the ship's galleys (kitchens). A tired deck officer, wearily beginning his 4 AM shift on the bridge, may not pay much attention to the constant symphony of annoying, early morning fire claxons, as he imagines them all to be caused by bakers opening their ovens in preparation for the day's batch of fresh bread. Slumped over the central fire control panel, the exhausted and often hung-over officer may simply hit the ignore button on his computer and make the biggest mistake of his life in doing so.

I hope cruise ship companies take note of the possibility of a terrorist attack seriously, and I urge deck officers to be more vigilant when dealing with flashing fire alerts on the bridge's central computer consol. Remember that young officers on a Caribbean run may be more concerned with getting drunk and having sex with someone's drunken wife, than dealing with fire alarms. They would just assume the alarms were activated by hair driers, or a cigarette, in a passenger's cabin, or caused by the flames searing a galley chef's brandy flambéed crepes.

Captains and first officers may be too busy navigating and manoeuvring the ship into a difficult docking position, with the assistance of a jabbering harbour pilot, to be bothered with routine alarms in the background. Officers may get into the bad habit of simply assuming there is an innocent explanation for a fire alert, and switch off the alarm immediately. Meanwhile an arsonist's fires take root in hidden corners of the ship, only to be taken seriously when it is far too late to extinguish them.

There is one more thing to consider. If you are thinking of a cruise ship holiday, and believe ship's security staff check everyone's luggage for guns or explosives, think again. There are, of course, brief checks at most ports and everyone coming into the ship must put their luggage through an x-ray machine, and walk through a metal detector. However, on a hot day in a busy port with about two thousand passengers to quickly herd onboard in order to sail by a particular departure time, there are always mistakes made. Moreover, whilst passengers may be checked, crew checks are limited and security checks for those delivering goods to the ship's stores are almost non-existent. A pallet of guns could be loaded onto a cruise ship, only to be later unpacked by a mutinous crew with a piratical agenda, and unarmed security officers would be virtually helpless to do anything about the situation.

So, whether it be for an act of piracy, arson or terrorism, cruise ships could be seen as floating targets awaiting their doom in these increasingly dangerous times. Obviously I hope I am wrong, but forewarned is forearmed.

Modern piracy is on the increase, especially in areas such as the Gulf of Aden, the Bay of Bengal and the South China Sea. Nearly $16 billion dollars is lost to pirates working in these parts of the world, mostly as a result of ships being boarded, and their passengers and crews being robbed or held for ransom. A lifejacket may soon be replaced by a bullet-proof vest, and flare guns may perhaps be used to ward off pirates rather than signalling a distress call. Pirates are back on the ocean waves, so terrorists will soon follow.

Today's terrorists use low-tech weapons in their asymmetrical war on civilised society, the establishment, America or the West. Why carry an AK-47 assault rifle when infecting a herd of cows with foot-and-mouth disease can threaten a country's entire food supply? Why accumulate a cache of explosives, when igniting a forest fire is more effective than blowing up just one building?

Don't be fooled by police, law enforcement and security services that convince the media that they protect your nation from terrorists because they use the latest explosive detection technology. All that a terrorist needs is a box of matches to cause havoc, destruction and death.

Moreover, it may be almost impossible to define and determine who actually is a terrorist until it is too late. With regard to Islamic fundamentalists who wear masks and face scarves, dress in military uniforms and wave banners advertising the name of their terror organisation, recognition of their violent maniacal status is easy. However, what about the nice Muslim doctor who treats your mother down at the clinic? Is he a terrorist? Does he have concern for his patients or is he secretly planning a campaign of death in the name of Allah?

Two Islamic terrorists were burnt to death in the Scottish city of Glasgow, in 2007, when they tried to ram a car full of explosives through the front door of Glasgow Airport. Their car burst into flames on impact with the reinforced glass door, and, luckily for the crowds of tourists at the airport, the ensuing fire did not spread throughout the building. The dead terrorists were doctors at a popular Glasgow hospital, and all their accomplices were found to be Muslim doctors working throughout the UK.

These terrorists wanted to make a dramatic statement and gain international publicity for their cause through TV news reports. However, in their role as doctors they could have been quietly and secretly injected patients with an AIDS infected serum instead of penicillin, or the plague instead of morphine, and anthrax instead of a mild sedative. Muslim terrorist chefs could poison the curries that they sell to infidels in restaurants, or they could steal your bank details if they work for any government agency with computer access to your personal information. They could arrest you and perhaps shoot you dead of they are policemen, or frame you for a murder you didn't commit.

The first loyalty of Muslims is to Islam; living in a civil society with infidels is a secondary concern. So forget looking for Al Qaeda and Osama Bin Laden; the nice Muslim chap next door could be the one to blow up your morning bus to work. Such things do happen.

But if we think like this then we will all be too afraid to leave our houses. We will fear all foreigners and shun those who look different from us and who follow a different religion or point of view. We will believe everything the news and the government tells us, and we will become even more divided and separated from our cousins overseas with whom we share the planet.

Yes, the nice Muslim man next door could be a terrorist, sure, but what are the chances? Slim! Not every Muslims is a terrorist, not every black man is a rapist, not every Columbian is a cocaine dealer, not every Ivy League graduate is an upper-middle class white-collar criminal.

Anyone could be a terrorist, but we have to use our common sense in dealing with those whom we suspect or fear, and simply hope that we don't become a suicide bomber's next victim.

When the evils of the world were released from Pandora's box, all that remained was hope. Let's not lose hope, too.

Chapter Four

DECEPTION IN SCIENCE AND NATURE

Because the dimensions of the Universe are unknown by humans, the deceptions that flourish in the realm of science and nature may be infinite. Indeed, our understanding of the subject of science and nature is, of course, hindered by the limitations of our own intellectual ability and physical senses.

The deception here is that, in theory, the academic pursuit of science has the potential to explain everything (not that scientists have ever made such a wild claim). In fact, scientists are actually struggling to explain anything! From the first electron to the end of the Universe and everything in between, science is a mixture of guesswork, custom, coincidence and luck.

Exact Science

In the 6th Century B.C., Thales of Miletus began to disentangle the mysteries of the Universe and life, without necessarily requiring the existence of gods to add weight to his theories. Thus, philosophers ventured forth on their journey towards scientific discovery. However, such methods of understanding life split into two distinct camps, the rationalists and the empiricists, who viewed the world with separate monocles.

Under the leadership of René Descartes, rationalists preferred to doubt everything until they calculated its meaning by using innate powers of reason. Descartes even doubted his own existence until he concluded that the very fact he was thinking about the problem was proof he existed; "Cogito ergo sum" ("I think therefore I am"), a clever but erroneous conclusion. The "Cogito," whilst proving the existence of thought, does not prove that a thinker generates his own thought, merely that a thought is being generated. The concept of "self," therefore, is the product of either the supposed thinker's mind or of another separate thinker, perhaps God. Thus the conclusion, "I am thought, therefore I am" is more accurate, although most people would not describe themselves as being a "thought" or the product of "thinking."

Empiricists such as John Locke, on the other hand, felt that we are born with a mind like a blank slate ("tabula rasa") and that we have no innate ideas. Essentially, Locke was suggesting that everything we know is the product of our experience, calculation and learned values.

However, both the rationalists and empiricists recognised that the world about us can deceive our senses, and that we can even deceive ourselves about empirical data if we are handicapped by poor education, prejudice or the assumptions made from a distasteful experience in the past. Furthermore, the path to understanding life and the Universe is further hindered by deception present in the natural world, as well as the realm of scientific discovery.

In such an unknown Universe can we really say there are so-called "exact sciences," or those disciplines that leave little or no room for error in continued discovery once a scientific principle or law has been established (through experiments and rigorously tested hypotheses)? Are maths and geometry exact sciences? This is a question to which most scientists and mathematicians will give an affirmative answer. They will tell you that the calculation $2 + 2 = 4$ is self evident and a tautological truth, that is, if we understand the semantic definition of each particular element of the statement.

$2 + 2 = 4$ because 2 cannot be something else at the same time as when it is called "2." So a scientist will conclude, therefore, that a thing cannot be two different things at the one time. Yet if that is the case why do electrons have both wave and particle qualities at the same time? If scientists cannot imagine a place in the entire universe in which $2 + 2$ may equal 6, a metaphysical philosopher certainly can.

Perhaps there is a life form somewhere in the Universe that divides its body and reforms again at such a rapid speed that it is would be difficult to count it as either one life form or two. But we don't need to search too far for a creature that is neither one nor another of something. Humans may consist of a body and a soul, so we ourselves could be both spirit and matter at the same time. I mean, when we refer to ourselves as "I" or "me," we are not referring to just our soul or just our body, we are referring to their union, under the guiding influence of the "mind."

I am well aware that "2" is just a numerical concept, and a philosophical and linguistic definition of something that may or may not exist in the real world or in our imagination. However, I am suggesting that we should be cautious when assigning a concrete and unchangeable nature to a number. I am also well aware that outside a drunken philosophy argument in a student union bar, we have to assume a concrete and unchangeable quality in numbers in order to catch the number 12 bus home.

Putting labels on things is very risky for scientists and mathematicians, as nothing is certain in this crazy universe. Just when we think we know something, something else comes along to become the exception to the rule.

Of course, our struggle with scientific discovery is made harder when the definitions of terminology cannot even be agreed upon. Bizarre as it may seem, American English has changed the definition of a mathematical term and has, of course, produced much confusion over the years. The definition in question concerns the word "billion," meaning one million millions, rather than its new Americanised value of one thousand millions. Of course the word required by Americans in this instance is "milliard," not billion. To assist Americans with their continuing struggle with the English language, the rest of the world now uses the term "billion" to mean one thousand million, and the original definition has now been abandoned.

In other areas of science, a geometrician will say that a triangle is a triangle no matter which point in the Universe one finds it. This is conceptually true, yet a triangle is never a triangle when it is represented physically, be it drawn on paper, on a computer scene, or crafted as a wooden "A frame" underneath a house's slate roof.

The problem is that no perfectly straight line can be drawn by any implement or tool, at our current stage of technology. Microscopic flaws in a graphite pencil line will of course result in a myriad of angles being added to such. It may appear to be a straight line or a perfect triangle, circle or square to the naked eye, but it is not. It is not perfect and not exact if the definitions of such words are to mean without any flaw and are the best example of something in existence.

And speaking of definitions, is a triangle correctly defined as a shape with three angles and three sides? I mean, if you look at a triangle drawn on a piece of paper, you can count three angles inside the shape and three angles outside the shape. So any time you draw a conventional three-lined triangle it, in fact, has six angles and six sides. Thus an accurate semantic definition, for that which is regarded as beyond question and constant, is another problem for exact science.

With mathematics the problem with being inexact does not stem from irregularities in precise calculation, for in maths if calculations are precise there should be no irregularities. However, the mathematical offshoot of statistics can indeed show irregularities. Undeniably, statistics can be absolutely infested with falsehood and deceit. This situation has gained especial notoriety ever since Benjamin Disraeli uttered those famous words: "Lies, damned lies and statistics."

Market researchers have used statistics to show the popularity of a service or product, whilst politicians have used statistics to both support a party manifesto, or to defame it. The world's governments are often quick to use statistics to prove to the public that they are doing a good job for their respective countries, when in actuality many of their official statistics are feeble attempts to disguise ineptitude. Lets take the democratic world as an example.

In the largest democracy, India, a general election that saw 50% of the nation expressing their right to vote would perhaps seem a tragic affair. Only half the county bothered to vote! But 50% of India's population is nearly 500 million people, and a huge voter turnout, thereby yielding an enormous political mandate for the winning party.

But let's take the matter even further. In the UK, if 50% of the population voted in a general election, about 30 million people, and 50% of those who voted backed the winning party, it would mean that the British Government was voted into power by only 15 million out of around 60 million people— the deception of indirect democracy being that it is indeed democratic. In this case, the majority is told what to do by the minority, thus defeating the purpose of true democracy. However, we should also remember that not everyone is eligible to vote in a General Election, either because they are unable to do so (children and those under 18 years of age, the mentally handicapped, members of the House of Lords, etc.) or because their name has been removed from the electoral roll (prisoners, those convicted of electoral fraud, etc.).

When it comes to political elections, many people in the West labour under the misconception that electoral fraud and corruption are only found in African, Asian and South American countries. Sadly, electoral fraud can be found everywhere there are elections, in every country in the world.

Aside from being remembered as an incompetent, immoral and incoherent warmonger, American President George W. Bush will also be remembered for being elected to office as a result of electoral manipulation. Despite rival candidate, Al Gore, successfully winning the 2000 presidential election, George W. Bush's team of devious minions quite likely changed the outcome of the election results in the key state of Florida.

With Bush's brother, Jeb, as Florida State Governor, and also with Catherine Harris as supervisor of elections and head of the Bush for president campaign, 179,855 votes were not counted. Of these votes, 53% were cast by African Americans, most of whom backed Al Gore for president.

With Bush winning the Florida vote by the thinnest of margins, only 537 more votes than Gore, it is obvious that instead of a legal battle to include spoilt ballots and the votes of those who were illegally disenfranchised, the entire Florida ballot should have been rerun.

Of course, we should also remember that it is not in fact the American public who ultimately vote their country's president into office, but "Electors" in the Electoral College, who simply take the outcome of the popular vote in each state as a guide to whom they should send to the White House, based in large part on awarding electoral "points" that are assigned for each state. Moreover, if there's no clear winner decided by the Electoral College, then the decision goes to the House of Representatives.

George W. Bush became president because of a dubious manipulation of numbers. But the Bush administration may not be so pleased about all the "numbers" that his terms in office have produced. For example, the number 1,422 is the amount of people who died as a result of the flooding caused by Hurricane Katrina, which devastated New Orleans. President Bush was heavily criticised for his complete lack of support for both the families of the victims and for the 1.5 million Americans who were made homeless by rising floodwaters.

Another number: 33,000 (approximately), is the amount of US military personnel who have been wounded in armed conflicts in Afghanistan and Iraq during the time George W. Bush was president, with an additional number of approximately 5,000 killed.

Perhaps Bush should also be associated with the number 666.

When gathering information for statistical analysis, the wording of questions can sometimes lead respondents into giving ill-thought answers, or at least bring confusion to a target population. Moreover, if someone is asked to complete a multiple choice questionnaire or survey, and find there is no option that suits their opinion, the overall statistical picture will be affected. Indeed, the very timing of a poll or survey may also influence the results.

If a poll is conducted during a freezing winter that poses the question, "Do you like a hot drink before going to bed?" a positive response will be high. The same question asked in an especially hot summer will obviously not invoke the same response.

Descriptive statistics can also prove to be a source of deception and misleading information, especially with regard to expressing details of central tendency. The problem here lies with the erroneous picture that the mean, median and mode create, when taken out of context with their relevant use.

For instance let's take the arithmetic average of a group, or the numbers of a set added up and divided by the number of scores, known as the mean. If three people wanted a small hat size and three people wanted an extra large hat size, a calculation of the mean would probably conclude that a medium sized hat would be the most suitable for everyone involved. When, in fact, such a hat would be too big for some people and too small for others, and not suitable at all!

The measurements of central tendency known as the median—middle number, and the mode—most common number, are also confusing. If an alien designer was drawing up plans for a human cage for his zoo, and only had statistics to go on, the median and mode may be truly unhelpful.

If his extraterrestrial scouts had observed a group of humans and had concluded that the middle height of such beings was five feet, that would be fine for men under five feet, but terrible for those six or seven feet tall. Of course, the general problems and deceptions created by central tendency are commonly rectified by using a standard deviation from the mean, but we should still recognise that not all numbers tell the truth.

Common sense would tell us that coconuts are less dangerous to humans than great white sharks, yet statistically more people are killed by coconuts falling on their head each year, than are eaten by sharks. So, statistically speaking, coconuts are more dangerous than sharks!

In the case of Earth sciences and astrophysics, a plethora of untruth and deception can be uncovered if one dares to investigate the matter. I say "dares" because of the restrictions to discovery with which religion once burdened scientists. Although natural philosophers in ancient Greece proved the Earth to be round, the Church still insisted that our planet was both flat and the centre of the universe. Galileo was nearly burned at the stake for suggesting otherwise.

The difficulty with scientific discovery and disclosure is that we cannot all be biologists, chemists, physicists and zoologists, and we must, therefore, trust such people to tell us the truth about our Earth and Universe in the simplest terms possible. Such trust has, therefore, led to blind faith in scientific discovery, a situation that enjoys little criticism from the common man. After all, if we do not understand something, or are completely unaware of its existence, how can we criticise it?

Yet things that we routinely teach our children at school deserve to be constantly revised, lest we perpetuate another "flat Earth." After all, it was not too long ago that some American states made it illegal to teach children that humans evolved from apes, and that humanity did not begin with Adam and Eve. Indeed, the "creationist" fantasy is still being told to unquestioning brainwashed children of the Abrahamic faiths of Judaism, Christianity and Islam.

It is rather embarrassing that some members of the human race actually believe the Biblical story concerning our creation instead of realising our obvious connection to the natural world, articulated scientifically by Charles Darwin's theory of evolution. Yet even today there are religious fundamentalists who simply refuse to accept anything other than the creationist theory and assorted myths concerning how the human race began. The situation is made even more ludicrous by giving credence to the philosophy of people such as the 17th Century Bishop, James Ussher, who used Biblical chronology to calculate that everything in existence was created circa 4004 B.C.

People who believe that the age of the Earth is less than seven thousand years old may also believe that dinosaurs did not exist, as they were not mentioned in the Bible. After all, Adam and Eve would surely have thought twice about leaving the Garden of Eden if there was a Tyrannosaurus Rex lurking in the wilderness. Such people think that dinosaur bones are either the result of God testing their faith, or that Satan is planting false "evidence" to suggest that the Biblical account of creation is nonsense. But anyone with a modicum of intelligence doesn't need Satan to help them come to that conclusion.

Knowledge

So what do we "know" and what do we think we know about our universal environment? The Earth is circular, America and Canada are collectively bigger than Africa, and the stars we can see in the sky actually exist and are not illusions. These are factual statements, right? Wrong! All these statements are false.

The Earth is elliptical and not exactly circular in dimension, being that it bulges at its equatorial radius, which is larger than the Earth's polar radius. Africa is larger than North America and Canada combined, but seems to be smaller on traditional Mercator maps. The same deception is also true of Greenland, which looks bigger than China; and with Europe, which looks bigger than South America.

The reason for such cartographic errors is that the once imperial powers who made maps of the World liked to overemphasis the scale of their own countries and empires at the expense of the poorer nations and former colonies—although Mercator himself would probably explain the situation by uttering some bovine manure about global perspective and angular calculations.

The third part of the statement that I have said to be false is that stars exist. Well, that's not entirely accurate. Stars exist, but our knowledge of this fact relies purely on our witnessing unbroken streams of light photons. Light can deceive us, and, therefore, can only be a guide to a vision of the way stars used to look years ago, and not as they may look still. For example, in a vacuum the speed of light is believed to be constant, travelling at 186,282.3959 miles per second or 299,792,458 metres per second.

This means that the light from the sun takes eight minutes to reach Earth. Therefore, the worse case scenario is that if the sun has just been destroyed, we will only know about it in eight minutes time—the time it takes for light to travel 149,600,000 kilometres, a long time compared to the hundred millionth of a second light takes to reach us from the opposite side of the street.

As we look further out into space to Alpha Centauri, we can see the star as it was 4.3 years ago, being that it is 4.3 light years away, or a distance of 40.678 million million km. But it, too, may not exist anymore, perhaps falling victim to a supernova, or having been sucked into a black hole. Moreover, our nearest galaxy, Andromeda, is seen as it was 2.3 million years ago. A lot may have changed since then.

Yet we don't have to travel the vast immensity of space to recognise that light can deceive us. Illusions known as mirages can be created in desert areas, where the appearance of water is produced by light refraction through rising layers of hot and cold air. Indeed, it is astral light's journey through the fluctuating temperatures of Earth's atmosphere that make stars appear to twinkle.

Aside from that which we do not commonly know about the Earth and Universe, there are also things that scientists choose not to tell us, be they suppressed facts hidden from view by dishonest scientists, institutions or governmental bodies. Such hidden facts, therefore, range from the fruit of human greed to the widespread cover-up of issues that hold importance to us all.

Examples of an individual's greed and deviance can be found in the life of Thomas Edison. Credited for being the greatest American pioneer of electricity and the advancement of the telegraph system, Edison held patents for hundreds of inventions. However, a great many of these inventions were, in fact, the brainchildren of other people who worked for Edison at the time.

The most unfortunate case of Edison stealing other people's inventions was especially prevalent in the case of Nikola Tesla. Born in Croatia in 1856, Tesla eventually found himself working for Edison at his Menlo Park Works, with many other enslaved boffins.

Tesla was a man of almost unbelievable genius, making advances in dynamos, transformers, light bulbs and high frequency electric coils. He even considered the idea of atmospheric conduction of free electricity. Sadly, Tesla's genius was used and abused by Edison and his business partners alike. Tesla thus lived out his life in relative obscurity, whilst he kept on inventing things such as fluorescent strip lighting and Alternating Current (AC). Yet as he did so, others kept on relieving him of the credit, and any financial profit.

Scientists and explorers often take the credit for discovering or inventing something before anyone else. It would, therefore, seem there is a great desire to be remembered as the original or the first to do something important, tempting many scientists into deception and trickery to achieve such a goal.

In 1922 Lord Carnarvon and Howard Carter claimed they had discovered the tomb of Tutankhamen, the great Egyptian King of 1360 B.C. Although this archaeological find unearthed a priceless coffin of solid gold, and other fabulous artefacts, both of the British Egyptologists had many years previously been found in possession of various pieces of Tutankhamen's jewellery, items that should have been found at the same time and place as his coffin.

Thus speculation has arisen that Carnarvon and Carter actually found the tomb twelve years before they officially reported it, enough time to rid the subterranean chamber of all the treasure that they could carry and transport to England without drawing too much attention to themselves.

In the world of science and academia some people are just born to be ripped off. In 1605 the man who claimed that "knowledge is power," Francis Bacon, was very keen to remove himself from such power. Not only did Shakespeare take the credit for several plays that Bacon and other great thinkers and writers had authored, Bacon's idea of preserving food by freezing it would also be ripped off by Clarence Birdseye over two centuries after his death.

Although the quotes of famous scientists and inventors can bring inspiration, they can also give us clues as to whether or not someone is being honest with us. For instance, Isaac Newton once said, "If I have seen further it is by standing on the shoulders of giants." It seems a very humble utterance, until we relate it to the debate on whether or not he stole the idea of differential calculus from Gottfried Leibniz. Is "seeing further" a polite way of excusing intellectual theft?

Space Invaders

Moving on from the information that individual scientists refuse to divulge, consider the following scientific fact which the governments of the world like to keep very quiet indeed: the Earth keeps having near misses with large meteors and asteroids!

Being rather important information, perhaps we should further examine that which could threaten all life on Earth.

Approximately 65 million years ago an asteroid or large meteorite smashed into the Gulf of Mexico, causing enough devastation to wipe out the dinosaurs and most of Earth's plant and animal species. Their extinction was the result of tsunamis, earthquakes, volcanic eruptions and the absence of sunlight, blocked out by thick clouds of dust in the atmosphere.

Therefore, if asteroids and meteorites can cause so much destruction, why do scientists feel that we should not be informed about them when they are hurtling towards Earth?

Perhaps scientists think the general public would be uninterested in an event such as the planet's destruction. Or perhaps the truth is that we can't do anything about preventing such an event from taking place, and, therefore, there would be no point in unnecessarily worrying the public.

However, there are certain details about our possible extinction of which we all should be aware. And depending on your view of things, they are details that will either put your mind at ease or make you think twice about official statements such as "the meteor posed no danger." Two thousand million years ago an asteroid hit Sudbury in Canada, forming a crater 125 miles across. Now that's dangerous!

The kind of meteorites, asteroids and comets that pose a danger are often found to be in an elliptical orbit, which situations them to approach Earth every 50,000 years or so. Indeed, 50,000 years ago an iron/nickel meteor or asteroid struck Arizona, causing a crater to be formed that was a mile wide and 600 feet deep. This impact collision produced the force of a 20 megaton nuclear bomb, or 20 million tons of TNT. And in 1908 hundreds of square miles of Siberian forest were destroyed by a meteorite exploding five miles above the ground, with the force of a hydrogen bomb.

So it seems the time has come again when we should start watching the skies for such rocky visitors.

On Monday the 7th of January 2002, a giant asteroid came within 370,000 miles of hitting us. But if this huge distance puts you at ease, consider the asteroid "Hermes," which passed the Earth at a distance of 200,000 miles in 1937. That's 40,000 miles closer to us than the Moon! Hermes was a mile wide and would have caused damage equal to the explosion of three hydrogen bombs, like those dropped on Hiroshima and Nagasaki.

In 2006 Earth had another close encounter, this time with an asteroid named "2004XPI4." Fleeting past our planet at 17km per second, it was estimated that if 2004XP14 had struck us it may well have wiped out a small country.

Still sitting comfortably? Well you shouldn't be, there are more asteroids capable of destroying any city on Earth than there are stars in the sky. Let's just hope they don't decide to pay our planet a visit in the near future.

However, do expect to see an asteroid named "Apophis" around the year 2036. This asteroid is essentially a 300 metre wide lump of rock and ice, yet unlike other space invaders, this one may well hit the Earth!

The Environment

Aside from the possibility of extra terrestrial projectiles smashing into the planet, we are also faced with the serious problem of ozone depletion. Yet even though the negative effects of global warming may seem obvious to some, the deception here is that some scientists are not telling us the full facts concerning the environment or intentionally spread disinformation. Others are telling the truth, and have been for decades, but they have often been simply ignored.

Its seems politicians steer clear of environmental concerns because they may include the loss of a multi-national's profits, and therefore investment in a country, and also the possible unemployment of certain sections of the electorate, particularly if they work in fossil fuel extraction or any other highly polluting industry.

Moreover, the media seem unconcerned with environmental issues because readership of the popular press does not seem remotely interested. Instead, the press likes to paint environmentalists as gay cannabis smoking hippies who like to wave giant placards outside government buildings and bang drums in an annoyingly unmusical fashion. In fact, an environmentalist is anyone who wishes that the planet was currently a healthier place to live, and a place where future generations will thrive and flourish without global warming and pollution.

Amongst the worst deceptions that scientists have authored in past years has been the wide cover up of the harmful effects of radiation and nuclear waste on the environment, and the people who have been cursed with leukemia as a result. However, we are all deceiving ourselves by ignoring the truth of how polluted this planet has become.

Be it global warming, pollution, the potential extinction of plant and animal species such as coral reefs, pandas and tigers, or simply the high amount of waste that we produce, it is clear that the Earth is a sick planet. High levels of atmospheric carbon and sulphur dioxide emissions from the burning of fossil fuels such as gas, oil and coal have resulted in a phenomenon known as the greenhouse effect. This phenomenon has aggravated a rapid global climate change over the past two centuries; in fact, it started around the time that the Industrial Revolution took place.

Agriculture and the sustainability of Earth's food supply may even be threatened by climate change. Whilst some parts of the world will experience drier conditions and even drought, therefore reducing crop yields, other countries will experience new, wetter and warmer conditions that will be ideal for agriculture. America's agricultural industry may thus be replaced in the global marketplace by China and Russia, therefore affecting America's political relationship with its old Communist enemies.

It is estimated that only a 1°C increase in global climate would be enough to shift northern hemispheric agricultural climate boundaries 200 to 300 kilometres further north.

However, agriculture may also be affected by mild winters failing to kill insects that will decimate crops the following summer and bring diseases such as malaria to parts of the world that did not previously have the problem. For example, Western Europe may experience a rise of African insect migrations.

Crops that are damaged by insect infestations will require a higher supply of pesticides to prevent further decimation. Top-soil, robbed of nitrogen by a drier climate and harsh weathering, will require higher amounts of fertiliser to sustain agriculture, while both pesticides and fertiliser run-off will add to eutrophication of coastal regions, river systems and other delicate hydrology.

Aside from the potential harm to human health from drinking contaminated water, algal blooms caused by eutrophication degrade coral reefs and mangrove swamps that are essential for the sustainability of marine life. Therefore, water polluted with insecticides and herbicides can have detrimental effects on the fish we rely on as a food source.

According to satellite data sources, polar ice caps have been shown to have decreased in area by approximately 10% since the late 1960's. Moreover, there has been a dramatic thaw and retreat of mountain glaciers across the globe, and a 40% decrease in Arctic sea ice. Rainfall levels, on the other hand, have risen, especially in the northern hemisphere, which has seen a 2% to 4% heavy precipitation event increase since 1950.

Over the next century, widespread coastal and river flooding will be caused by both precipitation (rain, snow) and a rising global mean sea level. It has been estimated by the Intergovernmental Panel on Climate Change that sea levels may rise by as much as one metre over the next hundred years.

If, indeed, the global mean sea level was to increase by as much as a metre, the increase would spell disaster for most of the world's major cities such as London, New York, Tokyo and Bangkok. Moreover, large areas of land such as coastal **Bangladesh** and the **Florida Everglades** would be swamped, causing millions of people to be removed from their homes. Low lying islands such as the Maldives may even be completely submerged, becoming an "Atlantis" for future generations of divers to explore.

Even if all CO2 emissions were reduced or completely halted, the effects of anthropogenic climate change would still be felt for decades to come. In the worst-case scenario, where greenhouse gas levels continue to rise, extreme changes in world geography may occur.

For example, a sustained climate warming of just 3°C, over thousands of years, would witness the melting of both West Antarctic and Greenland's ice sheets. This, in turn, would produce a global mean sea level rise of about 7 metres. This rise would have major implications for the environment, human settlement and the global economy, causing a worldwide exodus of people from coastal areas to inland locations high above sea level.

Indeed, a rise of only 2.5 metres would swamp most of Bangladesh, whilst a rise of 4.4 metres would put much of Florida underwater, including the cities of Miami, Orlando and Tampa. If all of Earth's polar ice caps, glaciers and ice sheets were to melt, the global mean sea level would rise by up to 70 metres. However, and thankfully, this scenario is very unlikely.

But it is not only global warming that is posing an environmental problem. High levels of pollution, be it of the atmosphere, rivers, sea or land, are also an environmental time bomb. Whether it be the burying of nuclear waste and the danger of radiation, overflowing landfill sites, dumping toxic waste and sewage into the sea, spilling chemicals into rivers, accidentally or otherwise, or the overuse of toxic pesticides, we are taking little care of our planet.

Moreover, as we continue to chop down rainforests, we are potentially ridding the planet of not only a vital source of oxygen production, but are also destroying the habitat of thousands of plant and animal species.

So what the hell is being done to prevent this catastrophe? At present, the main environmental strategies are currently geared towards the use and implementation of renewable "clean" fuels and technology, instead of fossil fuels. These new energies include hydroelectric power, wind turbines, solar panels, wave and tidal generators, biomass gas generators and geothermal energy.

But even here there is deception, as governments actually play down the potential of renewable fuels to prevent loss of profits from oil, gas, coal and petroleum sales. Moreover, few politicians really want to deal with the backlash of countryside protesters who are against wind farms, for example, as they are an eyesore.

In the UK the majority of electricity is produced from the use of fossil fuels, whilst nuclear power provides 24% of the country's energy requirements. However, renewable fuels can offer Britain a safer, more environmentally friendly solution. For example, biomass generators could harness the power of methane gas from animal dung or organic waste products, whilst Southampton could supply geothermal energy.

About 23% of the UK's energy requirements could be provided by estuarine barrier turbines, whilst about 20,000 wind turbines could supply an additional 20% of our electricity. Indeed, the wind power in Scotland alone is potentially greater than the rest of Europe put together. Hydroelectricity, both solar and micro-hydroelectricity, are some other options to consider.

As individuals, and as a society, we can take better care of the environment by being more responsible for our actions. After all, the world in which we live is essentially the world we choose to create. We can cut down on fossil fuel usage by reducing our energy needs.

We can reduce waste by repairing and reusing stock resources, or even recycling them. We can stop littering, dog fouling of pavements, and frown heavily upon antisocial crimes such as vandalism. In other words, we can try to cure the sick Earth by reusing more resources, and wasting and destroying less. Common sense must also prevail over greed.

There is no sense in chopping down a rainforest to provide grazing land for cattle that will be turned into cheap hamburgers. For what good is a cheap hamburger if you have no oxygen to breathe whilst you're trying to eat it?

Don't be fooled into thinking that caring for the environment and reducing the harmful effects of global warming is someone else's responsibility. It is your responsibility to do your part for the environment. It is also your responsibility to educate yourselves by finding out just what is happening to the planet. Every time you burn a pile of rubber tyres, or pour gallons of toxic chemicals down the drain, you are deceiving yourself if you think that it will all be okay. It will not!

Aliens
Aside from the gory details about the true state of the biosphere being kept from public view, scientists may also be hiding details of Earth's relationship with the rest of the Universe. Are we being deceived into thinking that we are alone in space?

If NASA does ever decide to spill the beans on their lunar ineptitude, they also might want to put an end to the speculation that they are in touch with alien civilisations. The Search for Extraterrestrial Intelligence (SETI) has been the subject of many Hollywood movies, but has failed to deliver an answer to whether we are alone in the universe or not. The SETI project has been refused vast sums of government money, either because scientists know aliens exist and do not have to keep searching, or that they believe alien life does not exist and it would, therefore, be a waste of time and money to continue the search.

Although it is a romantic notion to think that there are warehouses full of UFOs in Area 51, and that the U.S. Air Force is aware of sophisticated alien technology, it is more likely that aliens have not visited us in the past few thousand years, if at all. After all, if aliens were, themselves, interested in meeting intelligent civilisations, why would they come to Earth?

It is human arrogance to assume that we are intelligent and are at the peak of our evolutionary process, rather than just beginning it. For aliens to feel they must travel the vast distances of space to meet us, surely we would have more to offer than a world infested with violent warmongers, corrupt politicians, Islamic terrorists, obnoxious drunkards and dishonest criminals.

I cannot say whether so-called UFOs contain alien pilots or not, but what I can say is that it would be highly unlikely that aliens do not exist. The known universe contains 10 thousand million trillion stars; surely there is life out there somewhere. Our galaxy alone possesses 200 thousand million stars. Of these, 17 thousand million are capable of providing life-sustaining heat and light to approximately 600 million satellite planets.

So the question that we should ask is not whether aliens exist (of course they do), but why have they not contacted us? Perhaps in space terminology the Earth is regarded by aliens as a celestial "Billy No-friends." It might, therefore, be useful for humans to take a look at ourselves as a species, and ask who we really are and what we have to offer. If we don't, our world of deception may remain just that, our world, with ourselves alone.

The Natural Word
Scientists who pull the wool over our eyes are an annoying aspect of society, but are not as skilled in deceiving us as the natural world. Be it the product of God, evolution, or both, deception in nature can range from the simple and effective use of colour in animal mating rituals to the complicated production of chemical pheromones; from the luring trap of quicksand to the fairy light of Will-o'-the Wisp, all of which are both natural and deceptive.

Consider the three most important aims of animals and plants: to gain food and water, to procreate, and to avoid being killed. To achieve these goals, living creatures and plants have adapted special tools of deception in an attempt to turn the odds of survival in their favour. Camouflage, for instance, can be used as both a tool of evasion or as an aid to hunting—the leopard, trap door spider, death adder and stonefish being animals that use camouflage to a predatory advantage. Similarly, stick and leaf insects cleverly imitate plants to avoid being eaten by birds and spiders.

Some insects, rather than imitating plants, copy the appearance of insects that have either chemical protection, or an odour which makes them unpalatable to predators. Moreover, certain insects can even mimic predators themselves. Butterfly wings often bear markings that resemble the eyes of a bird or larger animal, whilst the wing markings of a South American "lantern fly" (*Fulgoridae*) have an uncanny resemblance to an alligator's head.

It is not only insects that use deception to their advantage, as there are brilliant and crafty hunters that lurk deep under the sea. One such predator is the angler fish. The angler fish is a benthic (bottom dwelling) species that employs a small and brightly lit bioluminescent lure, attached to the front of its head, to tempt small fish closer and closer to its gaping mouth—just like innocent teenage humans who are attracted to the bright and dancing lights of a big city, and subsequently find the dangers there.

Deception as an aid to procreation or pollination is also an ability mastered by animals and plants alike. Yet we needn't look further than our own species to know how important a deceptive appearance is in the mating game. One example of this is jackets with padded shoulders that help human males to look more muscular than they are.

The same trick is actually used by lions through having thick manes, which act a visual symbol of their dominant status within a pride. Male lions with thick black manes are especially attractive to lionesses. Additionally, in the case of bullfrogs, cockerels and pigeons, a puffed-out chest helps to attract a female mate. It would, therefore, seem that mating behaviour in the animal kingdom supports the notion that bigger is better.

As for plants, mimicry of insects can be an effective way of assuring pollination. Orchids, for example, can often produce structures that resemble female flies or wasps, whilst also emitting the odour of rotting carrion; a dream date for a fly. However, rather than such plant mimicry being just another fascinating aspect of nature, it may fuel the debate on whether or not there is a heavenly creator. After all, could evolution alone enable a plant to resemble an insect so accurately, without having a brain or eyes to guide such expert mimicry? Perhaps this form of deception hides the secret of creation itself.

Evolution made living organisms, plant and animals, but there may be a God who made evolution. In this case, perhaps this same God also tinkered around with his designs or gave a few creations a helping hand to reach perfection, so to speak. I agree with 99% of Darwin's theory, but hesitate to say that evolution was the sole creator of certain plants and animals, which display remarkably clever camouflage or mimicry.

Fauna and Flora

Sitting at the breakfast table we sip a milky cup of tea. We then put on our leather shoes and jacket and walk to the supermarket to buy something for lunch, a pink square of "steak" wrapped in cellophane, perhaps. We return home and spend the day in front of a computer or a large TV screen, imagining that we are not animals and that we live a distinctly separate existence from the Earth's fauna and flora. Have we forgotten that milk comes from cows, animals that also give us leather? Do we not remember that the pink square of beef was once a living creature that has died so that we may live?

When we see chimpanzees at the zoo we ignore the fact that human genomes are more than 98% identical to a chimp's and that we have an acutely similar DNA structure. When we find a cockroach running across the kitchen floor we panic and reach for a can of insecticide, failing to realise that, numerically speaking, this is an insect planet (unless, of course, you count micro-organisms like viruses and bacteria in the global census of species).

The point I'm trying to make is that, with the assistance of technology, we seem to be removing ourselves from the natural world when in fact such a move is impossible. Unless we are packed into a hermetically-sealed plastic box or are placed in cryogenic suspension, we constitute a part of the natural world around us and have a relationship with such.

We use plant and animal products for food, clothing, construction materials, medicine, furniture and decoration. Not forgetting our use of plants and animals for the simple and aesthetic pleasure of looking at beautiful things, such as a peacock, a butterfly, a bouquet of flowers, the plumage of a tropical parrot or a forest of autumnal-coloured trees swaying in the wind.

Therefore, we are making a big mistake and deceiving ourselves if we do not recognise the symbiotic relationship that we have with the natural world. In this relationship we must see that we have a responsibility not to abuse the Earth or to just keep taking more than can be replenished, whilst giving nothing back to the planet other than pollution, waste and destruction.

Humans can often be arrogant in their opinions about nature, and assume that because animals don't have computers, humans are superior and have the right to kill and destroy what we please. Humans also don't accept that animals can work with us, rather than simply being pets, pests or food.

But let's have a quick look at these points. To paraphrase Monty Python, "What have the animals ever done for us?"

Aside from being objects of curiosity, pets and food, animals also provide us with leather, suede, fur, feathers, bone, oil, musk, gelatine, fat, shellac, silk, wool, ivory, shell, pearls, lanolin, casein, ambergris, castoreum, carmine, sponges and manure, to name just a few.

In addition to being cruelly abused in vivisection and cosmetic research laboratories, animals can use their natural abilities to assist us. Horses and camels are used as modes of transportation, whilst oxen and elephants continue to do the jobs of a tractor or bulldozer in areas of the world where such industrial and agricultural vehicles are either too expensive or unsuited to the terrain.

Pigs track and sniff out truffles for their owners, whilst monkeys climb trees and throw down coconuts for us to eat. Snakes lie in oil palm plantations and prevent rats from devastating such by greedily devouring oil palm seeds. Meanwhile, dolphins help Navy divers detect underwater limpet mines attached to a ship's hull.

In Turkey and Japan small "doctor fish" (*Garra Rufa*) are used in health spas to nibble on the dead flesh of people with skin disorders and unsightly scarring on their bodies. The fish gently eat away at the areas of skin that may not have been helped my medicinal creams and conventional treatment, and have been reported to have worked wonders.

Dogs can replace the hearing and sight of the deaf, blind or visually impaired. They are also guards and protectors. They can help police officers by sniffing out a drug dealer's stash of heroine or a terrorist's explosives. Dogs can find skiers buried in an avalanche or those trapped by rubble in the aftermath of an earthquake. Dogs may even be used by doctors one day, as they have an uncanny ability to "smell" impending death and can detect cancer in the human body.

But you now may say, "Mr. Stanit, we know all about dogs and horses. They've been helping mankind since we emerged from the caves to build villages and establish civilisation."

To this I would ask, "And what of the insects, scavengers, dung eaters and other creepy crawlies? Do they help us in any way?"

Many people would cry out, "Eugh, yuuk! Creepy crawlies are horrible— of course they don't help us."

So the deception of fauna (animal life) is that many humans tend to think only of the animals that are in farms, zoos or pet shops as being helpful to our existence. Most animals help us in some way, directly or indirectly, even if they are only a part of the food chain or perhaps just a tourist attraction.

Of course there are exceptions; mosquitoes, rats and parasites have wiped out millions of people by spreading diseases such as malaria, bubonic plague and a host of other nasty ailments. However, not every insect or scavenger has such a lethal role upon the Earth.

Bees, wasps and other flying insects pollinate flowers and plants. Plants provide oxygen, food, medicine and wood. Bees also give us honey and Royal Jelly. Worms keep soil aerated, eat bacteria and produce humus and organic residues. Without the lowly worm and other unsung ground organisms, grass would not grow on the soil. No grass, no cows. No cows, no hamburgers. No hamburgers, no rich, fat and greedy Americans. Yes folks, without worms, the "Big Mac" would not be possible. And without the Big Mac, America may grind to a halt.

The "creepy crawlies" and scavengers that most of us dread and despise also perform the function of eating dead fauna and flora and recycling it to enable new life to flourish and grow. Without maggots, crows, cockroaches, vultures, flies, worms, dung beetles and the other detritivores that eat organic matter, the world would be littered with dead animal carcasses and mountains of soggy brown leaves.

So-called "creepy crawlies" may also provide doctors with invaluable assistance in hospitals. Following on information from military reports of soldiers who noticed their wounds were kept clean and sterile by maggots, hospitals treating patients with gangrene are now employing "maggot therapy" to kill harmful bacteria that has built up a resistance to antibiotics.

Leeches have also returned to the world of medicine, and are used to assist in amputee surgery. If, for example, a patient's severed fingered has been reattached to their hand, a leech may be used to ensure a fresh supply of blood is drawn through the finger, accelerating the healing process.

Even with all our fancy technology, for doctors to still be relying on leeches in the 21st Century surely tells us that, firstly, humans are not as clever as we like to imagine, and secondly, that we should respect animals for their own "technology" and natural abilities.

If we collected all of the secret technology and futuristic inventions assembled by geniuses at NASA, the CIA, MIT, SONY and Oxford University, we would still have nothing to rival the natural abilities of animals.

For example, a snake can not only see heat and track any warm-blooded animal, but it can "taste" the tiniest movement of its prey by flicking out its tongue and analysing the dispersal of scent particles in the air.

A bat uses "echolocation" with its vocalised radar system to track small insects for food, whilst whales and dolphins can communicate with each other over vast distances using sonar "beeping" language.

Sharks can smell one drop of blood in a million drops of water, whilst bloodhounds have a sense of smell that is tens of millions of times more sensitive than any human or, indeed, our "electronic nose" technology.

Hawks and eagles can see four times better than a human, and whilst we have binoculars, telescopes and camera lenses to magnify distant objects, the eagle's eyesight still gives it a superior depth recognition and colour perception.

Finally, if you ever doubt that the animal kingdom cannot match human technology, just take a look at any domestic cat. A pet cat has amazing physical abilities that the world's military can only dream of mimicking one day. What vehicle do we have that has the relative speed, strength and power of a cat? What robot can speedily climb up a tree, squeeze through the smallest of spaces, and always land the right way up if it falls?

What soldier is as stealthy and as cunning as the feline hunter that purrs on our lap? What can bite, rip and tear an enemy to pieces with the same merciless ferocity as a cat? A cat has superb eyesight and night-vision, far better than military "starlight" technology. Moreover, if anyone has ever seen a cat just sitting and staring at something invisible, you could almost believe they can see ghosts, too.

In conclusion, humanity should not continue to deceive itself by thinking that we are in some way superior or removed from the rest of the natural world. We are animals, and as such should have more love and respect for the other life forms with which we share this planet.

I'm not suggesting that we become vegans and live on water and rice, instead of eating a big juicy steak for dinner. Nor am I suggesting that we should stop throwing a stick for a dog to fetch as it is demeaning and not encouraging the use of all its natural gifts. No, I am simply saying that when we allow the rape and devastation of the natural world, and the destruction and abuse of Earth's fauna and flora, we are actually kicking ourselves in the teeth.

Fauna and flora do not sell drugs, start religions, commit acts of genocide, peddle child pornography on the internet, or destroy the global environment. Just remember what your species is capable of before you happily pat yourself on the back for being human.

I'd rather be a cat.

Chapter Five

DECEPTION IN RELIGION

If you are religious, then you are deceiving yourself, and indeed have been deceived.

You will find this chapter to be one of the shortest in the book, not because religion is free of deception, but because I have devoted a whole book to the subject, titled *Religion Must Die*, which I urge you read.

Religion is one of the most disgusting inventions ever to crawl from the minds of men. It is a sure sign of insanity and the banner of the corrupt and depraved. Religion is a dog chasing its tail, chasing a phantom, going round in circles. Religion is the medal proudly worn on the chest of the ignorant and timorous. It is the quicksand that engulfs the dim-witted and drags them into muddy peril.

If the mind is a ship and imagination the endless ocean on which it sails, religion is the anchor that prevents the vessel from leaving shallow waters, to explore the unknown with the power of reason blowing in the sails.

I am a deist. I have a rational understanding of God, based on reason, the experience of life, a sense of spirituality and everything I have ever read or heard about on the subject of a deity existing. For most deists, "God" represents a Universal force, a higher collective consciousness of all life, perhaps the initial creator of all things, the answer to the unknown. The deist God may be the entity that first created life, but which has taken no further action towards manipulating the creation. Therefore, the deist God does not answer prayers, perform miracles or dictate laws, commandments and absurd books to mortals. The deist God is not cruel, nor is he/she/it/them kind. The deist God is not vengeful nor is he/she/it/them loving. The deist God is everything in existence; essentially, we are the deist God, or at least a part of it.

A rationalisation of God's existence is not the same thing as belief in such, which is simply accepting something without question, as religion offers. But don't confuse religion with a rationalisation of God. Religion is a man-made creation designed to control the savage masses and relieve them of their money, freedom and intellectual abilities. The deist rationalisation of God is an attempt to understand life, creation and the universe, without the restriction of religious doctrine and illogical propositions to hold back the mind.

If you want deception, open the doors of any church, temple, mosque or synagogue.

It is said that people should have the freedom to worship their God in whatever manner they choose. In theory this is correct. There should be freedom of speech and thought in human life. However, when the religious begin to restrict the same human freedom that allows them to worship, then we should all be concerned. The religious kill members of rival faiths. They bomb the innocent with the name of a God on their lips. They order women to be subservient to men and to cover their bodies' exposed flesh. They chop off the foreskin of baby boys and the labia of baby girls. They call themselves "the chosen ones" and look down their noses at the rest of us.

Religion is harmful to us all. Religion has caused wars, hatred, bigotry, murder, torture, genocide and terrorism. Religion must die!

Consider that if God wanted us to be religious, there would only be one religion and one holy book in existence, and God would have written it himself!

I say again, if you are religious, then you are deceiving yourself, and indeed have been deceived!

These are statements that will infuriate many people with deep religious opinions, and yet are statements which should not to be dismissed solely because of their un-politically correct nature.

If freedom of speech is a reality in today's society, those who suggest that they or their leaders are in communion with God should also be prepared to accept the opinions of those whom believe God has made no such communication. The first deception of religion is, therefore, that it says that we should criticise that which is morally, ethically or spiritually "wrong," yet it refuses to be criticised for being "wrong" itself.

To list all deception linked to every religion requires a far more extensive study than is found here; therefore, this chapter merely serves as a brief introduction to the subject of the three great monotheistic religions of Judaism, Christianity and Islam.

Religion, the abominable cornucopia of lies, is a device that humanity should either recognise as a complete sham, or a tool to gaining power over the masses.

Just as we abandon the belief in the tooth fairy or Santa Claus in childhood, so should humanity abandon the belief in religion being a path to God, if such a being exists. Quite simply, it is time for humanity to grow up, join the world of reality, and to put away the talismans and trinkets of our ignorant and superstitious past.

Karl Marx and Niccolo Machiavelli have given us some of the most convincing reasons why we should denounce religion as nothing more than a weapon of political manipulation, or a bludgeon of social division. Claiming religion to be "the opium of the people," having both soporific and addictive qualities, Marx pointed out that humans of prehistory attributed supernatural powers to entirely natural phenomena, such as thunder and lightning.

However, instead of creating a useful theory that would bring meaning to human existence, early religious leaders simply used their self-elevated positions to separate themselves from the misery experienced by everyone else.

Consequently, the high priests of thunder gods or the spirits of the forest ceased toiling in muddy fields with the rest of the peasantry because such labour would be damaging to their "spiritual purity" and their ability to communicate with polymorphic deities.

It followed that the ignorant masses who believed such nonsense were forced to provide food, clothing and shelter for those who called themselves priests and holy men. A basic division of the upper and lower classes was thus invented.

Machiavelli, on the other hand, did not assess religion so much as being a divisionary tool in society, which reinforced class structure, but rather as that which provided power to those who could manipulate the beliefs in religion to their own ends. Popes, for example, have historically abused their position to gain wealth or political control. Machiavelli also suggested that a politician, or "Prince," need not be religious in actuality, just appear to be so, a suggestion made from the observation that religious politicians more easily gain public respect and trust than those who lead a more secular life.

In modern times, other great philosophers and people of note have tried to explain the folly of believing in superstitions and religious trickery, many of whom were desperate to prove the validity of genuine supernatural forces.

Master magician and escapologist Harry Houdini was heartbroken when his mother passed away, so much so that he spent the remaining years of his own life trying to contact her through spirit mediums and clairvoyants, a venture that proved to be the downfall of the spiritualist community in America and Europe in the 1920s.

Like his magical namesake before him, Robert Houdin, Harry Houdini made it his quest to uncover the plethora of charlatans and dishonest con artists infesting the occult fraternity at the time.

Being skilled in stage illusion and conjuring techniques, Houdini was famed for being able to recreate any spiritualist "miracles," much to the annoyance of fraudulent clairvoyants. However, his key to unlocking their initial deception was to ask mediums to give him any message that his mother had sent him from across the ethereal plain.

If such a message was successfully received by a medium, and was in fact addressed to Harry Houdini, the master magician knew he was being conned. His real name was Erich Weiss, and his mother never referred to him by any other name.

Despite the efforts of Houdini, Marx and Machiavelli to bring truth to the murky concept of religion and superstitious beliefs, people remain as attracted to religion and magic as a moth to the flame.

Yet the reasons for this fatal attraction, at the expense of common sense, are obvious. It is an integral part of human desire to understand the universe, and if a religion or facet of the occult can provide the answers, then they will be welcome.

Furthermore, not only will a religion explain the reason for existence, it will probably make a guarantee with the faithful that if they believe in religion they will go to heaven when they die. If they do not believe, they will fry in the agonising depths of hell for all eternity, suffering the rectally inserted prongs of Satan's trident as an additional discomfort.

Ministers, priests, mullahs and rabbis will all prefer that their loyal flock listen obediently to sermons, rather than scrutinise the written and spoken word with a fine-tooth comb. Indeed, in the Bible's case, this had only been the privilege of those educated few who could read Aramaic, Hebrew, Greek or Latin, the English translation of the Bible, as we know it today, being less than five hundred years old.

One last thing, if I get my wish and religion dies, what then? Man invented hell to threaten us with everlasting punishment if we stepped out of line. So what will happen if people suddenly realise that hell doesn't exist, and that there will be no punishment awaiting them after death? Will everyone run amok and unleash anarchy upon the Earth?

This is a question we must answer, sooner rather than later. I am confident that one day humanity will arise from its intellectual slumber and realise the folly and falsehood of religion. On that day we had better have a backup plan; a rule of law in a civil and enlightened society with real rewards and punishment, rather than fairy stories about heaven and hell.

I look forward to the dawn of our intellectual awakening and the birth of a rational planet.

Vatican Villains

Of the entire World's gurus, mullahs, rabbis and evangelical priests, none are so vile as the popes who have literally burnt their names into history. Holy men popes are not, hypocrites they most certainly are.

If popes are to condemn to the fiery pit of hell one in every ten men on Earth for their homosexuality, their own morals and behaviour should be beyond reproach, which is not the case. So perhaps it is time to re-evaluate a pope's value, both to the Christian faith and to humanity itself, by taking a brief look into the history of this religious leader throughout the ages.

Ever since Saint Peter proclaimed himself to be the first Bishop of Rome in 42 A.D., popes have ruled the Catholic world in some form or another. They have held roles as spiritual leaders to the followers of Christ and as power hungry tyrants who showed little mercy to heretics and non-believers.

You may believe that the head of the Catholic Church is a gentleman who would not even harm a fly if it landed on his mitre. However, the late Pope John Paul II has been responsible for much heartache surrounding the problem of contraception. In parts of the world where Catholic AIDS sufferers are dying in their thousands, the order not to use condoms is wholly unwelcome.

Moreover, Pope John Paul II could have been described as being a hypocrite, condemning the rich and famous for wearing diamond encrusted crucifixes instead of giving money to charity. The pontiff obviously forgot about the vast hoard of priceless art in the Vatican museum and of the overflowing coffers in the Vatican Bank, not to mention the jewel encrusted alter paraphernalia found in most churches. All this treasure could be sold to alleviate world hunger and poverty, and could fetch a far greater price at auction than a pop star's diamond crucifix.

John Paul II also made it a mortal sin to read horoscopes in the morning paper, as they are the product of occult practices. The pope apparently forgot about the Magi cult or the Three Wise Men who supposedly followed the Star of Bethlehem to find the infant Jesus.

But John Paul II is by no means the worst hypocrite that the Catholic Church has ever inflicted upon us. As far as the real bad boys of the papacy go, the following are a few rouges from the Vatican's past.

Pope Gregory IX and Sixtus IV were the guys who ordered the European inquisitions to rid the land of anyone who was not a Catholic. Such inquisitions resembled the goriest "Hammer House of Horror" film when they got to Spain, giving Tomas de Torquemada the power to burn hundreds of people at the stake, after a street procession known as the "Auto de fe"(Act of Faith). Moreover, the inquisitors utilised such holy implements as thumbscrews, hot pincers, the rack and various crushing mechanisms to torture their victims into admitting their heresy, before they were burned alive.

The English Pope Adrian IV and Pope Boniface IX were both known as vicious despots who enforced discipline with a rod of iron. Clement V tried to kill off the Knights Templar because they had more money than he did, whilst John XXII accumulated a vast amount of treasure before kicking the golden bucket. Clement VII was cunning; Paul III was a womaniser who had two bastard sons; and John XII died of debauchery.

Pope John VII, better known as Joan to her friends, is regarded by the Church as fictitious. It seemed no one had bothered to check whether John was a girl or a boy, and as a result the pope apparently gave birth on a procession around the Vatican, a route that has never been repeated since. Even though the Church denies such an event took place, it is the case that every new Cardinal who is elected pope must sit on a horse-shoe shaped seat to have it confirmed that they possess testicles. The pope has balls!

However, of all the popes who have ruled throughout history, by far the worst was Alexander VI (1431-1503), who was so devious and amoral that Machiavelli based much of his political theory of gaining power on Alexander's unashamedly dishonest antics.

Not only did Alexander introduce censorship laws that would later ban Machiavelli's books, but he also fathered Cesare Borgia, murderer and despot. On the eve of Cesare's wedding to Princess Charlotte D'Albret, the Pope threw a party that would have impressed even Nero or Caligula. Every cardinal on the guest list was given two whores to keep them company whilst 50 naked dancers ran about on all fours, trying to collect as many strewn nuts as possible, using all orifices to do so.

The winner of the nut contest was then rewarded with jewels and silk, before an all out orgy took place that would make porn legend Ron Jeremy blush. Alexander VI eventually became the victim of his own scheming nature, however, when he drank a cup of poisoned wine intended for one of his friends at a dinner party.

All this said, the days of the pope being the Emperor are long gone, and it is true to say that John Paul II did some good work over the years. However, there still remains the question of the Vatican's involvement in backing Mafia corruption, and the Church's investment in companies that manufacture armaments. So perhaps the next time you watch the pontiff on TV, waving at the crowds of cheering pilgrims beneath him, ask yourself these questions: Is the pope a good man? And does his religion have anything to do with God?

Currently the pontiff and vicar of Rome is Pope Benedict XVI (a.k.a. Joseph Alois Ratzinger), a German who was trained by the Hitler Youth organisation to shoot down aircraft belonging to the allied forces during WWII. Therefore, aside from his loyalty to Christ and the Church, Pope Benedict XVI has also sworn his loyalty to Adolf Hitler and the Third Reich.

Obviously the young Ratzinger had little choice over his membership in the Hitler Youth. In Nazi Germany you either joined the gang or you were shot. However, I'd also suggest that the powerful Nazi brainwashing techniques, which Ratzinger would have been exposed to, would have shaped the current pope's philosophy and way of thinking. Yet I'm not sure which is the bigger lie and popular slogan of the brainwashed, "Hitler is our saviour" or "Christ is our saviour."

For me, the Hitler salute is as equally deceptive as the sign of the cross.

Infidelophobia

Having lived and worked in Islamic countries over the years I have found Muslims to be some of the most friendly, hospitable, trustworthy, honest, fun loving and reliable people whom I have ever met. The majority of Muslims are law-abiding citizens who care for their families and friends, and enjoy the fruits of a rich and colourful culture.

However, for all the positive things I can say, there are also two negative things about Muslims which should be a cause for concern by everyone else—two little niggling worries I have, which may just be the result of my own general hysteria about religion and paranoia about fundamentalists.

The first worry being the unshakable lack of trust which Muslims have in the cultural, academic and business aims and philosophy of Jews, Hindus or Westerners. The second cause for concern being the Muslim absence of ability to question or doubt Islamic faith in any shape or form.

Let's talk about freedom of speech. Whenever someone dares to publicly denounce Islam or make a derogatory comment about the prophet Muhammad, angry Muslims congregate in their thousands and protest in the streets, burning flags and effigies. They chant that "God is great" and that the person who caused the offence should be punished or killed. And in the worst case scenario, they actually follow through on the threat and commit murder in the name of Allah.

But I wonder if a single member of these chanting masses has ever stopped to imagine, even for a millisecond, that they may be the ones causing offence. Perhaps Islam is offensive, as it represents human ignorance and is a sign that we are far from being civilised or enlightened. Perhaps deists and atheists view the Muslim "call to prayer," heard booming from mosques five times a day, as a more sickening, stomach-churning noise than finger-nails scraping across a blackboard.

After all, to the sane and rational amongst the human race, Islam and every other religion on the planet offer us no evidence that anything they say is a fact. So if someone were to criticise the Jedi religion, for example, as being a fantasy and devoid of any proof that Yoda was in communion with a higher "force," this should be a welcome criticism, as it is obvious that Jedi knights are no more closer to God than anyone else.

"But Mr. Stanit, the Jedi leader Yoda is fictional, the Prophet Muhammad was real," you might say.

Perhaps, but were Muhammad's encounters with the Arch Angel Gabriel real? Did Muhammad really have the power to move mountains? Did he really tear the Moon in half and reassemble it again? Did he really fly to Paradise on a human headed horse? Or are these tales, reported by Muslims as facts, simply as fictional as anything Yoda and Luke Skywalker ever achieved?

But what if those who call themselves Jedi started to demand more rights and protection of their faith? Would you be concerned? What if your neigh-bours taught their children that Yoda was a real person, and not the green muppet-cousin of Kermit the Frog? Would you be concerned for the educa-tion and welfare of their children? What if fanatic Jedis began to blow up nightclubs in suicide bomb attacks, screaming "Yoda is great" before they killed a hundred innocent people? Would you be concerned?

Of course you would be concerned! But would you say anything about it, or would you be afraid that a bunch of thuggish Jedi knights would show up at your door waving light-sabres and demanding a sacrifice to the Jedi Council?

The point is that those who are not religious may regard Islam as having an equal status to the religion of the Jedi, viewing them both as products of fantasy and human imagination and not as divinely authored connections to God.

Therefore, the very existence of these religions would be seen as being insulting to human intelligence, and should of course be in receipt of constant and continual criticism. Unless of course we all decide to return to caves and give up all ambition of growing intellectually and spiritually. Religious tolerance is a concept dreamt up by stoned liberals who imagine that religious leaders have the best interests of their kneeling flocks in mind, rather than their money. A rational society should crush with a sledgehammer blow the concept and idea of religion—all religion, every one—good, bad and ugly. I'll give a kiss goodbye to Zen with a regretful tear in my eye if it means the acrid flames of Christianity, Islam, Judaism, Mormonism and all the other diseases of the mind are snuffed out and extinguished forever.

But that is not how the world works. People are terrified to speak up against Islam or any other religion which has devotees who are willing to die in order to kill. Freedom of speech is being threatened by the actions of religious fundamentalists, and is an extremely depressing situation for the few mortals who know for a fact that a religion's claims of divine authorship is a fantasy.

Let me ask you a question. Would you be happy if a temple of "Malis" was constructed in your town? Malis is the religion of the vengeful god "Halla," whose prophet was married to many women, one of whom was a child under the age of ten (six when she was betrothed). He was a prophet and tribal leader who was thought to have killed many men in battle, and who told his followers to keep women in a state of subservience and to have their hair, faces, limbs and bodies covered up in public. A man who perpetuated a religion which encouraged the hatred and mistrust of homosexuals and infidels, and demanded animal sacrifice to God.

Moreover, how do you feel about the followers of the Malis religion who have been responsible for brutal political regimes, human rights violations, terrorist attacks all over the world and who have murdered tens of thousands of people over the last few decades, all in the name of Halla and his prophet.

Again I ask, would you be happy to see a Malis temple in your town and would you be content to listen to the call to prayer at the Malis temple five times a day? Or would you call the police?

Well sadly you can't call the police because the religion is protected by law, and its name is not Malis but Islam, and its Prophet is Muhammad.

Freedom of speech allows Muslims the right to build mosques and to be legitimate and legal members of the global society. However it is inside these mosques that Muslims pray to a god who apparently hates homosexuals, Hindus and Jews. A god who will not welcome infidels into a heavenly Paradise upon their death. A god who rewards terrorist martyrs with the sexual pleasure of deflowering virgins. A god who demands the subservience of women to men. A god who needs the removal of foreskins and vaginal labia from those who are forced or choose to believe in him.

Muslims have the freedom to praise such a god, and yet many fundamentalist Muslims do not allow critics of Islam the same rights as they enjoy. A person would be risking his life if he dared to say that it is both obscene and illogical to say God hates homosexual, Hindus and Jews. Or that it is a painfully unenlightened human idea that sex should be a reward for anything, and is totally lacking in divine inspiration.

No matter how strongly we feel about something, we should all be prepared to consider the possibility that we are wrong and have made a mistake about our philosophy or faith. Many Muslims are unwilling to consider that they have made a mistake, and are therefore not champions of the freedom of speech given to critics of Islam.

On September 30th 2005, a Danish newspaper called "Jyllands-Posten" published twelve cartoons depicting the Prophet Muhammad in various guises. The cartoons were not flattering and were critical in nature, but were seen as a valuable and necessary part of the debate on censorship and criticism of Islam and religion in general. However, as the cartoons were reproduced in other newspapers across Europe and the rest of the world, the fury of the Muslim backlash grew to gargantuan proportions.

Instead of seeing the cartoons as thought provoking, or at least as an obvious and predictable expression of opinion on Islam by so-called infidels, Muslims condemned them as being blasphemous and demanded the head of the cartoonist. Not only were the staff of the Danish newspaper issued death threats, Danish embassies in Europe and the Middle East came under violent attack, and the usual flag burning ceremonies by chanting crowds of "holy" and "peace loving" Muslims followed.

The cartoons of Mohammad may well have been offensive, but they may also be as equally offensive as a mosque or a Muslim woman wearing a face veil. It's all just a question of perspective.

In 2007 a 54 year-old British primary school teacher, working in the African country of Sudan, was arrested for allowing her young pupils to name their classroom teddy bear "Mohammad." She was charged for breaking the strict Islamic country's blasphemy laws and faced six months in prison or forty lashes. After a brief spell in prison the woman was sent home in disgrace, shaken, but thankfully unblemished by whip or machete.

I have a question for the Sudanese police who arrested the kind old teacher. Is it blasphemous to name a building after Mohammad or a mass murdering terrorist? Perhaps the parents of terrorists called Mohammad should be arrested for their blasphemous act of naming their violent child after the Prophet.

It so happens that the name "Mohammad" is the single most popular name in the Muslim world, and I cannot see how naming a child's toy with this ubiquitous name can be blasphemous. Indeed, the teddy bear is an object of love and fond admiration, not an object of loathing or a direct satirical lampoon of the real-life Prophet of Islam. Perhaps in Sudan love is blasphemous. One would certainly draw that conclusion on examination of the African country's record on human rights abuses.

Continuing the idea of perspective on religion, as a deist I still get a shiver up my spine when someone sends me a Christmas card each December. The sender obviously did not mean to offend me by posting out the greeting card, and were simply trying to wish me well. But they also did not consider that I may feel that the glittering representation of a baby in a manger, or three kings following a star, would make me unhappy, as I see religion as a step backwards and a hindrance to enlightenment. And it is the same for Muslims. They just cannot accept that Islam may not be such a good thing after all, and continue to pray, build mosques, cover women in veils, cut off foreskins, and kill innocent people in bloodthirsty terrorist attacks.

This brings me to the term "Islamophobia," or the fear of Islam, irrational or otherwise. As Machiavelli pointed out, we fear that which we don't know, and eventually this fear becomes hate. So those who suffer from Islamophobia probably don't know much about either Islam or Muslims, and therefore their fear is based on news reports of terrorist attacks and the hearsay of racists and members of other religions. They fear Islam because they don't know it and their fear soon turns to hatred of the religion and its followers.

However, there are those who have studied Islam and know Muslims and may still fear and even hate the religion, for a different reason than Islamophobia. They may conclude that it is not the fear of Islam, but the Muslim fear of Infidels which is a problem for the whole planet to worry about, Muslims included.

Therefore "Infidelophobia" is a more accurate way of terming one of the reasons for the current climate of fear and standoff between cultures of polar philosophies.

In my own experience of Islam I have encountered days when I was extremely frustrated that my Muslim friends and colleagues would simply refuse to consider what I had to say, if it was in any way derogatory or doubtful of the Qur'an and the Prophet of Islam. Indeed I was driven to despair on other occasions when I had outlined a scientific impossibility or philosophical dead-end in Islam, only to be told "we are not allowed to question this."

I simply could not understand how otherwise intelligent people could tell me that they could not and would not even try to ask questions about the stickier points of their faith. Yet perhaps they simply did not want to play "Jenga" with their religion, fearing that if they pull out one brick from the tower's base, the whole thing would collapse.

Of course some existentialists would support my Muslim colleagues in their hesitation to question matters of faith. After all, life is short, and if we need religion in our lives, if it makes us happier, if society is better with it than without it, fine—pick a religion and get on with life. Don't question what cannot be known, for this will only bring misery.

Yes, I understand all that, but what about common sense and the rational process of solving problems, religious or not? Even if we are not in the position to answer big questions yet, those questions should still be asked. Sheep should always ask if there is a way to defeat the wolves, even if there are no sheep who can give the answer. For if the question is never asked, bloodied fangs and slaughter will last forever.

For nearly two years, when I lived and worked as a teacher in a Muslim country in a very strict Islamic boarding school, I was told many weird and wonderful things which forced me to bite my lip to avoid uttering any bitter expletives. Let's have a look at just some of the arguments, statements and stories which I was faced with, and you can make up your own mind as to whether I was right to be shocked.

I asked a friend the hypothetical question, What would he do if his brother converted to Christianity? My friend replied that he would have to kill him. I thought my friend was joking, but he absolutely assured me that if any member of his family were to abandon their faith in Allah, he would be compelled to kill the traitor.

I concluded that Muslims are forced to surrender their will to God, and if they choose to do anything else they will be given hell by "merciful" Allah and a bullet from their family or friends. So even if a person who is born a Muslim but eventually, through good education and experience of reality, discovers that Islam is nonsense, they cannot live with their family and friends in a Muslim society. Unless of course they keep the truth of their new belief unspoken and continue to visit the mosque just to keep the peace and avoid unnecessary difficulty in their lives.

I imagine that there are people of all religions who are in the same situation. They know religion is a joke but cannot abandon it completely for a variety of reasons. In my own family there are Christians who know Jesus Christ was not God, his son or even his messenger. However, when a birth, death or marriage comes around, off they go to church, simply because it is customary.

Personally, I try to avoid entering churches whenever I can. Churches (temples, mosques and synagogues) are dark monuments of ignorance and bastions of perversion and insanity. Although some of their architecture and artwork is nice.

Once I mentioned to the head teacher of the school that I had read *1001 Arabian Nights* by Sheherazade. She told me she had never heard of the book. I then explained that it contained famous characters such as "Sinbad," "Ali Baba" and "Aladdin." She nodded in recognition of these names, but was not altogether impressed. I continued the strained conversation by mentioning that one of the first English translations of the book was completed in 1885 by the explorer Sir Richard Burton (not the actor once married to Elizabeth Taylor).

Again, the head teacher was not impressed. So I played my ace by telling her that Sir Richard Burton was also one of the first non-

Muslims to enter Mecca, disguised as an Arab. This final piece of information triggered an emotional eruption to rival Vesuvius. She ranted and fumed that "Allah would never allow such a thing" and that it was blasphemous to suggest otherwise. She told me that not only would God refuse to let infidels into Mecca, but also that the prayers of infidels are neither heard nor answered.

I know infidels are not legally allowed to enter Mecca and may be killed by "non-violent" Muslims if they try. But the giant hand of God did not reach down from heaven to prevent Sir Richard Burton and Sikh Guru Nanak from doing so. Perhaps Allah doesn't mind the occasional visit from an infidel.

When talking to a teacher of Qur'anic studies, I asked her what she felt when she prayed, expecting her to say that she felt relaxed and at peace. Instead she told me that she was in actual communion with God and that Allah spoke to her. This of course begged the question, what did he look or sound like.

The religious teacher paused before answering that she did not so much have a conversation in which she could hear God, but that she in fact became "at one with God" and communicated through the thoughts in her own head. However, when I asked her if being "at one with God" actually meant becoming God, she panicked and closed down the discussion.

Later I asked her where God was, and she told me God was everywhere. God is omnipotent (all powerful) and omniscient (all knowing) and omnipresent (everywhere). Yet if this was the case it would mean that in fact God is everything, and not simply present everywhere. Furthermore, if God is "everything" and we are "something," we are a part of God and therefore we *are* God, at least in some small way. For God, the whole is greater than the sum of its parts.

I demonstrated the idea of being continually connected to God by drawing a big circle on a piece of paper to represent God, a small circle to represent man, and a wavy line between them to represent the communion of prayer. The religious teacher was not happy with the big circle, as it was spatially limiting God's presence. A valid point, if God is indeed omnipresent, and not a giant deity who resides in a garden Paradise somewhere, such as the gods of Mount Olympus. But wait, what therefore is Paradise? We will come to that.

So I scored out the circle and said that the paper itself was God, as the paper represented everything, and that mankind shared the same paper. But she still didn't understand that there was only one sheet of paper, joined, whole and complete. If mankind was on the paper, and the paper was God and the universe and everything, logically, human beings are a part of "everything" too, and therefore a part of God.

No, this was blasphemous—Allah was perfect, whilst man was imperfect, the two cannot be joined, nor can man say he is God. The conversation was closed, this time for good.

Of course, someone may pick up this ball and run with it a little further. For example, if there is a god who is the creator, and he views us like a model ship inside a glass bottle, what connection does he have with us? The ship is not a part of its builder, it is a separate entity, right? Wrong! Thanks to sub-atomic particles and the very fabric of space, the ship is indeed connected to its builder, although the connection may not be visible or easy to detect.

Moreover, there is a connection of existence, either in a material reality or simply in the realm of thought. If I imagine an apple and a star, they are connected by their very existence in my mind. Furthermore, an apple and a star are still connected in our "reality" by the constant and universal soup of particle matter.

Space is not an absolute vacuum. It is not a collection of celestial bodies hanging in mid-air, disconnected in the void. Something material connects everything in existence.

Using the soup analogy, imagine God as an endless vegetable soup, which is not contained in a pot or bowl. Just an endless soup flavoured with intelligence and power, with a googolplex of ingredients, one of which is humanity. As one of the vegetable ingredients, we can claim to be a part of the soup and, in fact, cannot choose to be anything else. However, we cannot say we represent the entire soup itself. Nor can we, as a simple vegetable, say what the soup tastes like.

I imagine that when we die, going to "heaven" is the act of becoming a part of the soup's "stock" and Universal flavour. We will know more about the soup than we did as a mere vegetable existing from within its material nature alone, but still cannot claim to be the soup itself.

Thus, God is soup!

On the occasion of speaking with a councillor who had newly returned from the Hajj (holy pilgrimage to Saudi Arabia and Mecca), we got onto the subject of homosexuality. I, of course, said that gay people were just as much God's creation as anyone else and that science had proven that a person's sexuality is dictated by their genetic make-up and hormonal balance, not by choice.

Unsurprisingly, the councillor said that men were created to have sex with females and that gay sex was not natural. Moreover, that homosexuals had chosen to sin and disobey God's laws.

I brushed aside the "God's laws" notion, as no such laws exist, and is a matter of one's belief according to which religion one follows. However, I asked the councillor if she thought homosexuals were ghosts. She replied that I was being silly, and of course they weren't ghosts. Ghosts are "supernatural" entities, according to traditional definition, making human homosexuals "natural" beings which belong to our world of natural, everyday reality.

Homosexual sex was therefore natural, but perhaps not "normal." I didn't go into a detailed conversation about what I regarded as being normal in the bedroom as I follow the philosophy of saying that between consenting adults, anything goes! And that whilst normal sex is better than no sex, the idea of having "normal sex" sounds terribly dull.

I asked the old councillor what advice she gave to the homosexual boys at the school. At first she denied any gay boys existed in such a strict Islamic institution, but following a dozen examples of boys who were not exactly butch and who had an obsession with clothes designing and drama, she conceded that some boys may not have been "normal."

Because I taught drama I said I was very happy for this fact, as "normal" is boring, and boring actors kill a play.

She explained to me that the only advice she could give a gay boy (she didn't concede that lesbians existed) was that he was sinning against almighty Allah and would need to pray and ask God for advice.

She went on to say that AIDS was punishment for being gay. A truly disgusting idea. However, I said that if that was true, why then do innocent "normal" straight people get AIDS? Anyone can get AIDS, a child could accidentally stand on a junkie's infected needle and get the disease, a woman who needs a blood transfusion after a hospital operation or childbirth could get the disease if the blood she receives is infected. Anyone who has sex without using contraceptives (prophylactics) could contract AIDS.

If God was so petty and unforgiving that he really wanted to punish a "guilty" mortal for simply following his natural instincts, then surely such a mighty god could devise a disease which would only affect those whom he wished to punish, and not just anyone, guilty or not! But the followers of the Abrahamic god tend to lack imagination, with regard to what their god can do.

They say God can do anything, yet he relies on fallible mortals to ghostwrite his books through dictation to scribes and apostles, instead of writing them himself. The Abrahamic god cannot simply snap his fingers and rid the planet of sinners or infidels, he needs to employ mortal soldiers to fight "holy wars" and asks terrorist martyrs to kill in his name. The god of Abraham cannot answer the prayer of an amputee who wants a limb replaced and grown on his body once again, nor can the god of the Jews, Christians and Muslims stop tsunamis, earthquakes or global warming.

The councillor crossed her arms and asked me to leave her office.

There was no sympathy or understanding there. Actually, for a so-called councillor she was rotten at her job. If a young student came to her office, depressed and feeling gloomy because they were homesick or being bullied, she would say that Allah had chosen them to attend the school and that they should be grateful for the blessing. In other words, "Shut up and go away!"

I've encountered many such people in the Muslim and wider religious community over the years—people who hate homosexuals because a book tells them to do so. I wonder what they would do if a book told them to love homosexuals? Jesus said "love your enemies" but nobody seems too bothered with that piece of wisdom. Jesus wasn't a Muslim! No, but Muslims regard him as a messenger of God's divine truth, yet they don't listen to his message. After all, Muslims love to cast stones. Especially if an unfaithful wife is in view.

Two science teachers once had a brief conversation with me regarding my opinion on the Qur'an as a science book. I had to inform them that the "science" contained in the Qur'an was not in fact inspired by Muslim thought, or indeed by God, but rather by the Ancient Greeks. Moreover, that although Greek thought had been incredibly insightful for its day, a great deal of Greek thought had been disproved or discounted by the time the European Enlightenment had arrived. Therefore, I did not see the Qur'an as in any way related to the world of empirical scientific discovery.

The science teachers scoffed at this and said that I had either not read or understood the Qur'an properly, or that I didn't understand science. Both of which were erroneous as I have read and re-read the Qur'an many times over, and also, that two of my university degrees are science based.

I asked them about evolution, and whether they believed Darwin's theory. I stated that I believed the theory, not because Darwin had exposed the struggle for life and the survival of the strongest and most adaptable species. I also don't believe the theory of evolution based entirely on the fact that chimpanzees share a 98.4% DNA sequence similarity with humans. No, I believe in evolution because its truth is so bloody obvious. Even chimps know Adam and Eve didn't exist!

How close we resemble our ape cousins; how close our ape cousins resemble monkeys; how close monkeys resemble possums; etc., etc. On Earth, animals are all connected to each other in some shape or form. Moreover, species are in a constant state of change, in an attempt to better suit a constantly changing environment. Nothing living remains the same for too long.

We don't need to look back in history over a million years ago to recognise the changes in our own species, *Homo Sapiens*. Children all over the world are getting bigger and fatter than they ever have been since the dawn of our "modern" history, 130,000 years ago. Moreover, the "selective breeding" and "inbreeding" of blonde-haired Nazi children, muscular African slaves and the horse-toothed royalty of the world have proven that human beings can change their phenotype (physically observable characteristics) in the space of only three or four generations, never mind thousands.

Therefore, I do not believe the creationist theory of Adam and Eve as it is essentially, well,… total and utter bollocks!

However, the science teachers at the Islamic school where I worked were adamant that Allah had put a dark-skinned man and a woman, who spoke Arabic, on the Earth to populate the planet. I quickly pointed out that if God had wished to populate the planet, he would have created a billion Adams and a billion Eves, not just one of each. After all, in order to get the ball rolling Adam and Eve would have to commit incest with their children, or have it occur among the children, and their children would have to commit incest with the siblings and offspring, and so on.

With incest being a sin according to "God's law," how could any of us ever escape it under this scenario? Aside from this, geneticists highlight the proven dangers of such, and that continued incest will produce children who are deformed or mentally handicapped. This is a constant worry for European monarchs, being that most royal families are closely related to each other.

Moreover, if Adam and Eve were dark-skinned and spoke Arabic, how do Muslim scientists, who deny evolution, explain the fact that human beings have changed both appearance and language since then?

Of course any common sense examination of Adam and Eve will quickly lead a sane person to the realisation that it is a story invented to explain how we all got here, in the absence of scientific fact.

If Adam and Eve were really kicked out of Eden for eating an apple, what a totally unforgiving god must have created them! And as Adam and Eve walked away from Eden, I wonder what tools they had to fashion clothes with? And what food did they eat? How did they manage not to die of exposure and from all the disease which their immune system would have no defence against? Indeed, the survival of Adam and Even outside the garden of Eden is miraculous. How long would two naked people last today if they found themselves locked out of their luxury hotel, and wandering across the African Savannah, Arabian Desert or Australian Outback?

Would Adam and Eve have had to contend with dinosaurs? Probably not, because they were long gone by then. But do any religious creation stories mention them existing in earlier times? Dinosaurs are not mentioned in the Torah, or the Bible, or the Qur'an, so they didn't exist, according to fundamentalists from many faiths. But what about all these dinosaur bones we keep finding? They must be a Satanic trick to test our faith! But if dinosaurs and prehistoric life forms did not exist, how was oil formed? It is the same oil which Muslim countries make a fortune selling to the West.

Well, let's not ask any more of these questions, because the two Muslim scientists who had been talking to me left my company long before we got onto this line of questioning.

My point being, that fundamentalist religious teachers should not teach science unless both the religious theory and scientific fact are placed side by side, and are left for students to decide which makes the most sense.

Over the time that I worked alongside Muslims, we constantly chatted about the idea of heaven, or rewards in paradise ("jannah") and punishment in hell ("jahannam"). During the month-long fast of Ramadan I encountered a kind of "points for prizes" system, whereby my friends actually believed that if they fasted for longer than required, or at certain times of the day, they would gain greater rewards in heaven. Going to paradise was not good enough for them; they wanted to have even more benefits and privileges than the average Muslim soul.

The idea of a rewards system and tiers of privilege in a heaven of inequality inspired many chats on the nature of paradise. What is paradise? Where is it? No one could tell me where paradise was in the universe, be it in this dimension or another, or set in the material universe or the spiritual. I wondered, therefore, how the souls of the dead would find such a place if no one knew the way to get there.

For the many different ideas my Muslim friends had about paradise, and what rewards to expect, one thing remained constant—I would not be going there! As an infidel, I would join the ranks of the unwelcome and abandoned who would spend an eternity in the domain of torment and fire ("An-Nar"), the worst place to be.

So let's have a look at that point. On Earth there are around six and a half thousand million people (6.5 billion). Of this number, 33% are Christians, 20% are Muslims, 13% are Hindus, 6% belong to the folk religions of China and the Orient, 5% are Buddhist, whilst the remaining 23% of the population are members of other world religions, atheists, deists, or have their own philosophy about faith and God. This means that no-matter how good they were, no-matter how well-behaved, god-fearing, kind and considerate, 80% of the human race would go to hell. And that's just on Earth. But what of the millions, billions, or billions of billions of intelligent life forms in the Universe? They're all going to burn in hell with the infidels, if they are not Muslims.

Does it make sense for a creator and apparently loving god to make something just to end up destroying it, and even torturing it? Torture and punishment are human ideas and do not belong in a rational conversation about God.

If your children break the rules of the house, you don't punish them forever in a lake of fire. You discipline them, teach them what is right and wrong and get on with being a parent. Why would God do anything less? To say that hell even exists is to insult the idea of an enlightened divine force, which we call an omnipotent and omniscient God.

Which brings me to the point I made to my Muslim friends about heaven. If hell seems unlikely in the extreme, heaven, too, seems rather far-fetched. A place where all-out fantasies come true, a place where we are rewarded and loved, for all time, for eternity, for ever and ever, Amen.

I asked them if they were happy to live to the ripe old age of 99. They said it depended on their quality of life, but most agreed that they would be bored with life. The same old faces, the same old food, the same old routine. No-matter how nice things are, humans get used to them very quickly, and boredom sets in. Therefore, would we not all get really bored in heaven after the first few thousand years of driving a Ferrari around the clouds, and dining on venison and pheasant every night? Would we not be depressed after a million years of sex with 72 beautiful virgins, and perhaps conclude that there has to be something better? Something more intellectually stimulating perhaps?

The problem is that Muslims, like their cousins in the other Abrahamic religions, have a very Earthly idea of what a heavenly paradise actually entails. Again, as with every other conversation about such matters, my Muslim friends did not want to talk about paradise, as I was popping the bubble of fantasy and spoiling their dream of great rewards to come—a dream hindered by their own lack of imagination, itself a result of the limits of Muslim education.

We must all understand that the concept of heaven and hell was created to control the uneducated masses—to threaten them with horrific punishment if they broke God's law, which was also the law of the land and of the wealthy rulers, kings and emperors whom the people served. If the peasants rebelled against their rich and privileged masters, they would burn in hell for an eternity. Hence, this is why royalty and religion go hand in hand, together to the bank.

However, the same poor unenlightened masses were offered great rewards as a means of keeping them at bay, and for not rebelling against their life of misery and oppression. After death, heaven would be the eternal reward for those who obeyed, who didn't ask questions, who did what their church, synagogue, temple or mosque told them to do. How convenient, then, to offer great rewards to those who work as a slave in life, and will live like a king in death. It's funny that nobody has bothered to come back from heaven just to confirm this as being the genuine outcome of faith and loyalty, rather than a hilarious scam.

Some Muslims have taken the idea of doing what they are told by religious leaders one step further than most of us, however—for Islamic terrorists do what God himself apparently tells them to do. They are the honoured and cherished foot soldiers of almighty Allah and will enjoy especial rewards and pleasures in heaven.

Of course killing in God's name is easier than creating, healing, and saving a life in God's name. For example, the more extreme followers of the so-called "holy book" of the Qur'an have, since September 11th 2001, committed acts of terror in Indonesia, Chechnya, Iraq, Pakistan, Afghanistan, Thailand, Israel, India, Spain, Morocco, Russia, Nigeria, Egypt, Bali, the UK, and a number of other countries worldwide.

They have been shooting hostages, beheading people, bombing buses and schools, "honour killing" and mutilating Muslim women in relationships with infidels, killing children and murdering tourists. What brave and holy actions almighty Allah apparently demands. What incredibly civilised outcomes of his all knowing, all loving mercy. Allah Akbar, God is great!

Of course, God has *nothing to do with such atrocities* as they are the work of the criminally insane, deranged and deluded. In 2002 the "Bali bombers," for example, killed 202 people and injured over 300 more when their bomb exploded in a busy nightclub full of tourists. These crazy idiots were caught by the authorities and paraded in front of TV cameras with huge grins on their faces. They were so happy, so cheerful, so pleased to have taken the lives of infidels. They laughed and joked that almighty Allah was delighted with their work and that each man would soon die a martyr and meet 72 virgins in paradise.

The idea that God would reward murderers is a sick joke. The idea that God would reward murderers by giving them virgins to abuse and molest is an entirely human male invention, carved by the minds of those who are sexually naïve and inexperienced. Possibly virgins themselves.

And are 72 virgins enough women to last a sexually frustrated man for all eternity in heaven? Again, Muslims have not properly thought out their reward system.

Of the many Islamic education teachers at my school, one man in particular grabbed my attention, not least because he had two wives, leered at young girls, and made the occasionally inappropriate advance or comment to a female member of the staff. This school "holy man" was sometimes the subject of my inquiry into the finer points of his religion.

He asked me if I liked the food in his country, and I explained that I found spicy food to my taste. However, I was always unhappy to eat halal meat, as the animal from which it came was tortured before death. The holy man was baffled by this idea and assured me that all halal butchers kill their cows, chickens, lambs and goats by the quick method of cutting the throat with a very sharp knife. I explained that having the throat cut, and bleeding to death, was not humane nor was it as quick as Western methods of slaughter.

I continued by suggesting that both Muslim halal and Jewish kosher butchers may one day be closed down in a secular Western countries, which of course would lead to many problems for the Muslim and Jewish people who live there. However, it would not be sensible to continue a barbaric practise just to favour a particular religious group. Animal cruelty should be prevented at all costs.

He did not agree, as the rights of animals come second to human needs, and that the rights of infidels come second to Muslims. He did not comment on the Jewish position, or point of view.

In another conversation with the "holy man," we discussed the need for constant prayer. I commented that students seemed to spend a great deal of their time at school praying and reading and reciting the Qur'an. I put it to him that perhaps God did not need all these people praying to him so often.

I mean, why demand that mortals get down on their knees at all? It seems like an ego trip, and something which a human king, sultan or emperor may require to make them feel loved. But I don't think God needs his ego massaged with such genuflecting and obsequious, sycophantic bowing and scraping.

Do human parents need their children to worship them and to get on their knees five or more times a day? No, parents would tell their children after the first few times that they appreciated that their children loved them, but would rather they got off their knees and found a good job and made some money.

And what of prayer, anyway? Does it work? Assuming that listening to millions of prayers spoken five times a day, by Muslims alone, was not keeping God from more important matters, have any prayers even been answered?

We pray for God's help in so many trivial things. "Oh please God let me pass my Arabic exam," and when we are successful we give God the credit. "I passed with God's help." Yet if someone was to pray for something far more important than passing an Arabic test, nothing would happen. If a tsunami wipes out an entire seaside town, for example, no amount of praying will bring it back. If we lose a leg in a car crash, no amount of praying will bring it back.

Why not? God can do anything, right? After all, why would God help a spotty teenager pass his school exam, and refuse to grow another leg on a person who is in pain and suffering the indignity of being a wheelchair-bound amputee?

Deists would answer that whilst it is not impossible for God to answer prayers, as the creator can do anything he wants, it is unlikely that he would do so, as it would mean that God has an active influence on his creation, and that he is guiding and influencing our destiny. If this was true—that God plays an active role in manipulating human existence on Earth—then he must also take a great deal of blame for everything that is "evil," or which goes wrong on the planet. Therefore, it is logical to assume that if God exists, he plays no active role in human affairs and is simply an observer—a divine scientist watching a culture of bacteria growing and multiplying in a petri dish.

The Holy Man left me alone with my thoughts and went home to discuss Islamic self-restraint and the denial of animalistic pleasures with his two wives.

To conclude this brief look at Islam, I again want to say that the Muslims I have lived with, worked with, taught and talked with, have all been exceedingly nice human beings. They are people with whom I'd gladly share a vegetarian meal, a festival celebration and even the planet Earth itself. However, I have absolutely no desire to ever hear Islamic teachings or opinions again, simply because I find them distasteful and disturbing.

I have observed that the philosophy of Islam is unquestionably violent, brutal, oppressive and controlling. I have also observed that Muslim students are without doubt subject to what could only be called "brainwashing" rather than education. And it is fear, rather than love, which rules the lives of Muslims. Fear of God, fear of punishment, fear of disobeying, fear of other men leering at wives and daughters, fear of questioning the Qur'an, fear of Judgement Day, fear of the infidel, and fear of exploring and enjoying the pleasure of living!

The village or desert mentality and lack of worldly sophistication which many Muslims share leads them to distrust anything that Infidels have to offer. Therefore, science and Western philosophy remain as mysterious as rock n' roll and freedom of speech.

Young Muslim students are taught that they should never question the authenticity and authority of the Qur'an. If they have to pray morning, noon, night, before each class, after each class, before and after each meal, and at various other times throughout the day, when not chanting "Allah Akbar," when do they get a chance to think, to consider, to reason, to rationalise, to challenge what they are taught? The answer is never. They don't get that luxury.

I submit, therefore, that Infidelophobia will increase until somebody wakes up, smells the coffee, and presses the alarm button. We should all, Muslims and non-Muslims alike, realise that the gulf between different faiths and culture is not closing. So unless we all become deists, Muslims, or devotees of another crazy religion or philosophy, the world will keep its martyrs and its mistrust until someone can provide a shred of proof that their religion is something other than hateful and unhelpful balderdash.

Here's some advice from the most "holy" book of Muslims; The Qur'an:

"You shall fight in the cause of Allah."(2:244)

"Do not think that those who are killed in the cause of Allah are dead, they are alive, enjoying his provisions."(3:169)

"You who believe, do not take certain Jews and Christians as allies."(5:51)

"You shall fight back against those who do not believe in Allah."(9:29)

Did God really author and dictate these words to the prophet Muhammad? You decide. Personally, I think God doesn't need silly little mortals to fight battles between other silly little mortals, nor would he discourage the same mortals from being friends with each other. And as for fighting atheists, what does God care if people believe he exists or not?

Does the wind care if an eagle doesn't believe it exists, because it can't see it? Or does the wind carry the eagle to lofty heights, regardless of the bird's lack of faith?

God is great, Allah Akbar.

Chapter Six

CAVE EXIT

Well, there we have it, a veritable cornucopia of falsification, forgery, whitewashing, simulation, imitation, illusion and decoy. Be it the sham of religion, the deceit of sales and advertising, or the political and scientific manipulation and corruption of apparent facts, we simply cannot get away from untruth in this world.

This is a world of bluff; a world of disguise; a world of fraud and deception.

What you want to believe is up to you. I won't blame you for believing something even though you know it to be a lie; sometimes the deception is far easier to live with than the brutal truth.

Indeed, what fun would life be if there were no hoaxes and no deception to speak of? There would be no invisible flea circus at the carnival, no bearded ladies with false beards, no fake photographs of fairies, and no "Fiji mermaids" or any other amazing curiosities to marvel at.

Laughing at the money he was making from sewing the carcasses of fish and monkeys together to make a plethora of grotesque mermaids, circus impresario P. T. Barnum said, "There's a sucker born every minute."

Suspension of disbelief is fine at the carnival, but sadly there are people who are willing to believe all that they hear and see everywhere else.

However, if you are prepared to accept that the world is perhaps not quite as civilised as one would hope, not quite as shiny, not quite as evolved, but yet more beautiful than anything money could ever buy, walk out the cave exit.

Take a deep breath and walk out into the light.

Seek truth, for as Socrates once said, "The unexamined life is not worth living."

9 781585 091225